DON'T

GIVE

UP

▲ City
ON A HILL

Editing by Rachel Popham
Design by Nicole Enders

This journal is designed to provide encouragement when you are hanging by a thread, losing faith and short on strength. Find courage from Hebrews 11 and 12 and the heroes of our faith found in Scripture! Each day will include scripture, reflective questions, and prayer - all working together so you can cast your concerns on God and trust in his love and timing.

TABLE OF CONTENTS

WEEK

1

WEEK

2

WEEK

3

Day 1 | 18
Don't Give Up

Day 8 | 60
Desperate Moments

Day 15 | 102
All That Hinders

Day 2 | 24
The Cloud of Witnesses

Day 9 | 66
Keep Fighting: The Witness of Jacob

Day 16 | 108
Freedom from Anxiety

Day 3 | 30
Keep Believing: The Witness of Abraham

Day 10 | 72
Wrestling with God

Day 17 | 114
Longing for a Better Country

Day 4 | 36
Risky Faith

Day 11 | 78
Keep Perspective

Day 18 | 120
Looking Ahead: The Witness of Moses

Day 5 | 42
Redefining Faith

Day 12 | 84
Change Your Perspective

Day 19 | 126
Greater Than Treasures

Day 6 | 48
The True and Better Abraham

Day 13 | 90
Choose Gratitude

Day 20 | 132
Throwing Off What Others Think

Day 7 | 54
Reflection and Review

Day 14 | 96
Reflection and Review

Day 21 | 136
Reflection and Review

WEEK

Day 22 | 142
The Obstacles in Your
Way

Day 23 | 148
Keep Building: The
Witness of Nehemiah

Day 24 | 154
The Power of Lies

Day 25 | 158
Mission Accomplished

Day 26 | 164
Just Walk: The Witness
of Joshua

Day 27 | 170
Untangled From
Unbelief

Day 28 | 174
Reflection and Review

WEEK

Day 29 | 180
Take Heart: The Witness of
Gideon

Day 30 | 186
Take the Next Step

Day 31 | 192
Holy Fear: The Witness of Noah

Day 32 | 198
Keep Your Confidence in Christ

Day 33 | 202
Finish Well: The Witness of Paul

Day 34 | 206
Anchor for Your Soul

Day 35 | 212
Reflection and Review

INTRODUCTION

hen was the last time you were in a race?

Maybe you ran a 5K or even a marathon. Perhaps you were under a tight deadline for a big project at work, and the pressure was increasing as the finish line drew near. Maybe raising kids or serving your church feels like a marathon.

At what point in your race did you feel like packing it in, hanging it up, and calling it quits? When was discouragement most fierce? How did you respond?

Or maybe for you, the temptation to give up is more serious:

- You just received a cancer diagnosis.
- Your singleness feels like a curse, not a calling or a season.
- Your spouse is ready to end your marriage.
- You received another "not pregnant" message.
- You have just visited another explicit website.
- Your grown child has walked away from the faith.
- You don't know how you finished another entire bottle of wine.
- You love your special-needs child, but you're overwhelmed & exhausted.
- Your debt continues to grow, and no one knows you're in trouble.

If you find yourself in one of these situations, hear us out. You may want to hear the gentle, soft voice of Mr. Rogers, the neighborhood comforter. You may want to hear, "It's okay. It's not your fault." And those may be the right words for your needs.

But perhaps you need something stronger. In the words of Kyle Idleman in *Don't Give Up*:

"Sometimes, when we feel like giving up, we want Mister Rogers to come knock on our door—but we need William Wallace. Who is William Wallace? You saw *Braveheart*, right? ... He grabs you by the shoulder, and he says—he even growls—stuff like this:

"This is not the time to give up and go home! It's time to fight! Don't you dare back down! You're tired. You're discouraged. But don't give up!" (page 12 in *Don't Give Up* book)

So you don't really need the blue-sweater guy. You need the blue-face guy. You may feel the need for sympathy, but what you truly need is strength. You may appreciate a little genuine pity, but you need a kick to the posterior in the form of a challenge.

This study journal promises five weeks of posterior-kicking. I won't be harsh. I won't minimize your challenges. Quite the opposite. I want you to realize how daunting your situation is, how unlikely your success is, and how desperately you are in need, because that's where Someone Else can come through for you.

So don't give up.

What we need is real encouragement—a battle cry, a call to action, marching orders to push back the darkness. Stand up straight. Face your fears and enemies. And remember that you are not alone.

THE CLOUD OF WITNESSES

Where do we find such true encouragement for a long life of faith and endurance? In the witness of the saints throughout God's Story.

The author of Hebrews has written this to us:

> THEREFORE, SINCE WE ARE SURROUNDED BY SUCH A GREAT CLOUD OF WITNESSES, LET US THROW OFF EVERYTHING THAT HINDERS AND THE SIN THAT SO EASILY ENTANGLES. AND LET US

RUN WITH PERSEVERANCE THE RACE MARKED OUT FOR US,
FIXING OUR EYES ON JESUS, THE PIONEER AND PERFECTER
OF FAITH. FOR THE JOY SET BEFORE HIM HE ENDURED THE
CROSS, SCORNING ITS SHAME, AND SAT DOWN AT THE
RIGHT HAND OF THE THRONE OF GOD. CONSIDER HIM WHO
ENDURED SUCH OPPOSITION FROM SINNERS, SO THAT YOU
WILL NOT GROW WEARY AND LOSE HEART.

—HEBREWS 12:1–3

Have you ever recognized the power of these verses? What is this "great cloud of witnesses" that surrounds us—and how do they impart real-life courage to us today?

It is no ordinary cloud. This heavy, all-encompassing fog is a crowd of people. You don't see this kind of cloud; you feel it. The Living Bible translates the phrase like this:

SINCE WE HAVE SUCH A HUGE CROWD OF MEN OF FAITH
WATCHING US FROM THE GRANDSTANDS …

This cloud of witnesses gives us a powerful picture: A packed-house throng of history's greatest heroes watching you, cheering for you, calling out to you, "Get up! Keep going! You're almost there!"

In context, Hebrews 12, which starts with the transition word "Therefore," encourages based on the truths of Hebrews 11. Hebrews 11 is a famous chapter of the Bible that we often call the "Hall of Faith." In it, the author reminds us of the faith and endurance of our forefathers and spiritual mothers.

Noah—who built an ark based on faith in God's words alone
Abraham and Sarah—who left home and family to follow God to an unknown place
Jacob—who tried to run from his problems and found himself wrestling with God
Moses—who refused to let Israel be oppressed and led God's people to the promised land
Joshua—who simply walked in faith until the walls of God's enemies fell in a heap
Gideon—whose little army was empowered by an all-powerful God

.miah—who worked day and night to rebuild Jerusalem while surrounded by doubters
.l—who finished the race, kept the faith, and passed on to us the charge to build the church

These individuals were all witnesses of God's power and goodness to His people in the unlikeliest of scenarios. They all were pressed to their limits, hit the wall of desperation, and had to fight back the temptation to give up. And as a result, they experienced God's deliverance in historic ways.

These witnesses stand for you today; they cheer you on; and they call out to you in specific, tangible encouragements to keep going, keep believing, and keep the faith!

The crowd is chanting: Don't! Give! Up!

AN ENDURANCE RUN

My hope and prayer for you is that this journal serves as a guide on your long run of faith and spiritual growth. It's five weeks, but don't be intimated. God often called his people to forty-day journeys of spiritual transformation, and this five-week journal could enable life change that could last to eternity.

Consider making this more than just another book or another task to complete. Consider committing to a five-week spiritual endurance run!

This study journal has thirty-five days, including five days to catch up and review. That's thirty-five days saturated in God's goodness to his people throughout history!

TAKE A MARKER   TRACE OVER THE LETTERS

consider HIM WHO ENDURED such opposition FROM SINNERS so that you WILL NOT grow weary & LOSE heart

HEBREWS 12:3

The end of each day, you will find questions for your reflection. These questions are split into two categories, Content and Meaning & Meditation and Application.

CONTENT AND MEANING

The goal at this point is to ask of the text, "What does it say?" and "What does it mean?" The questions under the heading "Content and Meaning" will help you reflect on the passage along these lines.

MEDITATION AND APPLICATION

Now that you understand the passage's content and meaning, you will often do a second reading of the same passage. Why reread the same thing? Because to truly savor the depth of the passage and to begin to apply its message to your life, it takes deeper reflection.

The second reading is a "second-level" reading. Think of this as a level beneath the first reading. Rather than just looking at what the passage says and means, consider what it means for you today. So, as you read the verses again, read more slowly and thoughtfully.

The goal of this second reading is meditation—deeply engaging the truths of the passage with your heart, not just your head. Biblical meditation is not like Eastern meditation, where the goal is to empty your mind. Instead, biblical meditation is about removing distractions and filling your mind with the things of God. In biblical meditation, we slow down and center ourselves on his Word.

We read and reflect not merely to learn; we read and reflect to experience. God invites you to get to know him personally through his Word.

In the sections marked "Meditation and Application," you're going to be asking yourself, "What does it mean for me to obey this passage today?" and "How can I love and enjoy God more as a result of these truths?"

EXERCISE

BEFORE DIVING INTO DAY ONE, COMPLETE THIS SHORT EXERCISE.

WHAT DO YOU CURRENTLY DO WHEN YOU FEEL DISCOURAGED?

WHEN ARE YOU TEMPTED TO GIVE UP IN YOUR PERSONAL AND SPIRITUAL LIFE?

HOW DOES THE GOOD NEWS OF CHRISTIANITY INCLUDE AN ENCOURAGEMENT TO KEEP GOING, KEEP BELIEVING, AND KEEP WALKING?

WHAT IS ONE THING YOU WANT TO GET OUT OF THIS STUDY OF GOD'S GOODNESS IN HEBREWS?

HOW DO YOU WANT TO BE DIFFERENT AT THE END OF THIS STUDY?

THEREFORE, SINCE WE ARE SURROUNDED
BY SUCH A GREAT CLOUD OF WITNESSES,
LET US THROW OFF EVERYTHING THAT
HINDERS AND THE SIN THAT SO EASILY
ENTANGLES, AND LET US RUN WITH
PERSEVERANCE THE RACE MARKED OUT
FOR US, FIXING OUR EYES ON JESUS, THE
PIONEER AND PERFECTER OF FAITH. FOR
THE JOY SET BEFORE HIM HE ENDURED
THE CROSS, SCORNING ITS SHAME,
AND SAT DOWN AT THE RIGHT HAND
OF THE THRONE OF GOD. CONSIDER HIM
WHO ENDURED SUCH OPPOSITION FROM
SINNERS, SO THAT YOU WILL NOT GROW
WEARY AND LOSE HEART.

-HEBREWS 12:1-3

DON'T GIVE UP

KEEP BELIEVING

SINCE WE ARE SURROUNDED BY SUCH A GREAT CLOUD OF WITNESSES, LET US THROW OFF EVERYTHING THAT HINDERS AND THE SIN THAT SO EASILY ENTANGLES. AND LET US RUN WITH PERSEVERANCE THE RACE MARKED OUT FOR US.

—HEBREWS 12:1

DON'T GIVE UP

Not long ago, I entered a fifty-mile bike race. I hadn't been cycling long, and this was going to be the longest ride I had ever done.

I prepared well—months of training, stretching, marking out the route on GPS, and—my favorite part—carb loading. About halfway through the race, I felt great. I was going faster and doing better than expected, so I increased my pace above what I had planned. But around the forty-two-mile mark, the wind picked up, my water ran out, and every turn of the pedals felt like a struggle.

But that's when my help arrived.

Up until this point, I had been pedaling alone so I could keep my own pace. But now I needed encouragement, support, motivation—I needed another cyclist. Another racer and I had been passing each other back and forth over the past few miles, and he pulled alongside me and asked how I was doing. "I'm struggling! You?" He was struggling too.

Together we pedaled the final eight miles side by side. We didn't talk a lot, but we gave each other just enough support to keep going. We both wanted to quit, or at least take an extended pit stop at a fast-food joint, but we wouldn't let the other give up.

We finished the race side by side, thanked each other, and never saw each other again.

When I felt like quitting, when I thought I couldn't go an inch farther, I found encouragement in someone who understood my struggle and could stay with me until the finish line.

We all need this help. Someone coming alongside us, identifying with our struggle, and saying, "You got this! Keep going! Don't give up!"

ENCOURAGEMENT FOR THE RACE OF LIFE

Too often, I think of encouragement as a soft pat on the back for doing a good job. But Kyle Idleman, in *Don't Give Up*, gives encouragement some teeth.

"Encouragement is a battle cry. It's a call to move, to act, to advance. What kind of words accomplish that? To encourage means, of course, to give courage—to "speak courage into." That's not the same as making someone feel better. It's not patching up a wound but rather putting a weapon in their hands. It's giving them a fresh horse and the will to advance." (13)

The life of faith is a race, and it's not a sprint. It's a marathon. In fact, it's longer than a marathon—it's one of those ultra-marathons that those crazy people on television do.

In the ultra-marathon of faith, we need encouragement like we need food, water, and shelter. Where will we find this encouragement?

SCRIPTURE AND COMMUNITY

In the New Testament, the Letter to the Hebrews—written by an unknown author—speaks encouragement to the weary believers in and around Jerusalem. These believers were facing constant discouragement and persecution for their faith. Some were killed for their faith in Christ. Many more simply fell away when things got tough. But some stood firm.

How did these faithful Hebrews stay in the race?

the race of endurance, we see two elements we see most consistently: Scripture community. Again and again, the author of Hebrews points believers back to Old ment promises now fulfilled by Christ. And time and time again, he urges the to remain in relationship together and help one another through the long

At the beginning of chapter 12, the author writes:

> THEREFORE, SINCE WE ARE
> SURROUNDED BY SUCH A
> GREAT CLOUD OF WITNESSES,
> LET US THROW OFF
> EVERYTHING THAT HINDERS
> AND THE SIN THAT SO EASILY
> ENTANGLES. AND LET US RUN
> WITH PERSEVERANCE THE
> RACE MARKED OUT FOR US.
>
> —HEBREWS 12:1

We'll look at this "great cloud of witnesses" tomorrow. But for now, recognize that you will need the words of Scripture and the community of the church to run with perseverance the race marked out for you.

And this journal has been written to support your faith ultra-marathon.

We have designed this five-week study to be an endurance race of encouragement. We want to come alongside you and your friends. We want to call you to stand when others walk away. We want to shout, "You got this! Keep going! Don't give up!"

CONTENT AND MEANING

READ HEBREWS 12:1 AGAIN AND ANSWER THE FOLLOWING QUESTIONS.

IN WHAT SENSE IS THE CHRISTIAN LIFE LIKE A LONG RACE? CONSIDER THE FOLLOWING VERSES:

• "I RUN IN THE PATH OF YOUR COMMANDS, FOR YOU HAVE BROADENED MY UNDERSTANDING" (PSALM 119:32).

• "DO YOU NOT KNOW THAT IN A RACE ALL THE RUNNERS RUN, BUT ONLY ONE GETS THE PRIZE? RUN IN SUCH A WAY AS TO GET THE PRIZE" (1 CORINTHIANS 9:24).

• "YOU WERE RUNNING A GOOD RACE. WHO CUT IN ON YOU TO KEEP YOU FROM OBEYING THE TRUTH?" (GALATIANS 5:7).

• "I WILL BE ABLE TO BOAST ON THE DAY OF CHRIST THAT I DID NOT RUN OR LABOR IN VAIN" (PHILIPPIANS 2:16).

WHY DO YOU THINK THE BIBLE USES THE IMAGERY OF RUNNING SO FREQUENTLY?

WHEN HEBREWS 12:1 SAYS TO "THROW OFF EVERYTHING THAT HINDERS," WHAT DOES THE AUTHOR MEAN?

MEDITATION AND APPLICATION

READ HEBREWS 12:1 AGAIN SLOWLY AND ANSWER THE FOLLOWING QUESTIONS.

WHERE IN YOUR LIFE ARE YOU FEELING THE TEMPTATION TO QUIT? CONSIDER YOUR SPIRITUAL LIFE, FAMILY LIFE, FRIENDSHIPS, WORK, OR CHURCH INVOLVEMENT.

IF YOU COULD HAVE COURAGE POURED INTO THIS AREA OF YOUR LIFE, WHAT WOULD HAPPEN? HOW WOULD YOU LIVE IF YOU HAD UNLIMITED CHRISTLIKE COURAGE AND BOLDNESS?

WHAT ARE THE THINGS IN YOUR LIFE THAT COULD BE HINDERING YOUR RUN OF FAITH? WHAT SIN MIGHT BE ENTANGLING YOU? HOW CAN YOU "THROW OFF" THESE THINGS?

PRAYER

...AKE A MOMENT TO PRAY TO THE FATHER THAT HE ...OULD ENABLE YOU TO SUBMIT YOUR TRIALS AND ...ALLENGES TO HIM, FIND ENCOURAGEMENT IN HIS ...D, AND RUN THE RACE MARKED OUT FOR YOU.

THE CLOUD
OF WITNESSES

W hen was the last time you were in a big crowd?

A few weeks ago, I was at a college football game with sixty thousand other fans. Our team was facing the second-ranked team in the nation, and we were considerable underdogs. It was a close game, and although our team lost, our fans stood and cheered almost the entire three hours.

Why is it that we gather in crowds like this? It could be a community event, a rock concert, or even a wedding. There's strength in numbers, and we feel like we are part of something bigger than ourselves when we are in a crowd.

But have you ever been the source of a crowd's applause?

Perhaps you have to think back to singing or playing sports in high school, or maybe you have recently received applause for an award at work. If you asked me, "Would you rather have one thousand dollars or have everyone you know

DOODLE
HERE

stand and applaud you at once?" I would probably choose the latter. Maybe I'm vain, or perhaps in some deeper way we are hard-wired for this.

THE CROWD THAT IS A CLOUD

The Letter to the Hebrews paints this unusual, unexpected picture:

> THEREFORE, SINCE WE ARE SURROUNDED BY SUCH A GREAT CLOUD OF WITNESSES, LET US THROW OFF EVERYTHING THAT HINDERS AND THE SIN THAT SO EASILY ENTANGLES. AND LET US RUN WITH PERSEVERANCE THE RACE MARKED OUT FOR US, FIXING OUR EYES ON JESUS, THE PIONEER AND PERFECTER OF FAITH. FOR THE JOY SET BEFORE HIM HE ENDURED THE CROSS, SCORNING ITS SHAME, AND SAT DOWN AT THE RIGHT HAND OF THE THRONE OF GOD. CONSIDER HIM WHO ENDURED SUCH OPPOSITION FROM SINNERS, SO THAT YOU WILL NOT GROW WEARY AND LOSE HEART.
> —HEBREWS 12:1–3

This is no ordinary cloud. What is this "great cloud of witnesses" that surrounds us? Are they still standing and cheering today? If so, for whom?

In *Don't Give Up*, Kyle writes:

"The clue is in the word *therefore*, which points us back to the previous chapter. Hebrews 11 is sometimes called "The Faith Hall of ~~me~~." It offers a list of people who faced enormous challenges yet ~~d the faith to keep believing and the courage to keep fighting.~~

So those are the witnesses. But what's this about a cloud? Two different words are used for "cloud" in the New Testament. One is a single, detached, distinct mass of whiteness you see in the sky. The other—the word used here—is something wider and more powerful. It's an *encompassing* cloud, more like a heavy fog that surrounds us. You look up in the sky and see the first one. You *feel* the second one, around and enveloping you.

The ancient Greeks used that second kind of cloud to describe a crowd, a massive gathering of people. So in Hebrews 12 we have the idea of a huge throng of people all around us, wherever we go."(17–18)

The Living Bible supports the belief that this crowd of heroes is standing and cheering for believers today. It translates the phrase like this:

SINCE WE HAVE SUCH A HUGE CROWD OF MEN OF FAITH

WATCHING US FROM THE GRANDSTANDS …

This cloud of witnesses gives us a compelling picture: a packed-house throng of history's greatest heroes watching you, cheering for you, calling out to you, "Get up! Keep going! You're almost there!"

As Kyle notes, the language may be figurative or literal, but since witnesses are simply "those who see," we're invited to enjoy the inspiring idea that history's greatest heroes—Abraham and Joseph and Moses and David—are cheering us on.

In other words, look up. The crowd is chanting: Don't! Give! Up!

DON'T
GIVE
UP

CONTENT AND MEANING

READ HEBREWS 12:1–3 AGAIN AND ANSWER THE FOLLOWING QUESTIONS.

WHAT DOES THE AUTHOR OF HEBREWS MEAN BY A "GREAT CLOUD OF WITNESSES" ENCOURAGING TODAY'S BELIEVERS TO KEEP GOING AND KEEP THE FAITH?

WHAT IS THE "FINISH LINE" THAT THE AUTHOR ENCOURAGES US TO FIX OUR EYES UPON? WHY?

CONSIDER VERSE 3. HOW COULD JESUS WILLINGLY GO TO HIS DEATH WITH GREAT JOY? HOW ARE JESUS' DEATH AND RESURRECTION APPLICABLE TO US TODAY?

MEDITATION AND APPLICATION

READ HEBREWS 12:1-3 AGAIN SLOWLY AND ANSWER THE FOLLOWING QUESTIONS.

HEBREWS CALLS US BACK TO TWO THINGS IN OUR MARATHON OF FAITH: SCRIPTURE AND COMMUNITY (SEE DAY 1). HOW DO YOU SENSE THE LORD INVITING YOU TO WELCOME OTHER TRUSTED CHRISTIAN FRIENDS INTO YOUR STRUGGLES AND TEMPTATIONS?

HOW DO YOU RESPOND TO THE IMAGE OF A GREAT CLOUD OF WOMEN AND MEN OF FAITH CHEERING YOU ON IN YOUR DAILY LIFE? HOW WOULD YOU LIVE DIFFERENTLY IF YOU FULLY BELIEVED THIS AT ALL TIMES?

PRAYER

TAKE A MOMENT TO PRAY THAT GOD WOULD LET YOU SEE WHAT IS ENTANGLING YOU, ENABLE YOU TO FOCUS ON HIS SON, AND BE ENCOURAGED NOT TO "GROW WEARY AND LOSE HEART."

KEEP BELIEVING: THE WITNESS OF ABRAHAM

ebrews 12 begins with the word "Therefore." Do you remember the pun from high-school English class? Every time we find the word "therefore," we must stop and ask, "What is it there for?"

"Therefore" in Hebrews 12:1 points us back to the Hall of Faith in Hebrews 11. In other words, it's the "great cloud of witnesses" that offers us profound encouragement in our run of faith. It's the stories of Noah's ark, Jacob's wrestling with God, Moses's leading his people to freedom, and Gideon's little army.

These were all witnesses of God's power and goodness to his people in the unlikeliest of scenarios. They were all pressed to their limits, hit the wall of desperation, and had to fight the temptation to give up. And as a result, they experienced God's deliverance in amazing ways.

Let's start with the witness of Abraham: *Keep believing.*

ABRAHAM AND SARAH

Hebrews 11 records this about Abraham and Sarah:

> BY FAITH ABRAHAM, WHEN CALLED TO GO TO A PLACE HE WOULD LATER RECEIVE AS HIS INHERITANCE, OBEYED AND WENT, EVEN THOUGH HE DID NOT KNOW WHERE HE WAS GOING. BY FAITH HE MADE HIS HOME IN THE PROMISED LAND LIKE A STRANGER IN A FOREIGN COUNTRY; HE LIVED IN TENTS, AS DID ISAAC AND JACOB, WHO WERE HEIRS WITH HIM OF THE SAME PROMISE.
>
> —HEBREWS 11:8–9

Imagine what it would be like to follow God your whole life, get married, do well in your work, and reach old age. Imagine you're seventy-five years old, and you've lived in the same place since birth.

And now imagine God appearing to you and saying this:

> "GO FROM YOUR COUNTRY, YOUR PEOPLE AND YOUR FATHER'S HOUSEHOLD TO THE LAND I WILL SHOW YOU. I WILL MAKE YOU INTO A GREAT NATION, AND I WILL BLESS YOU; I WILL MAKE YOUR NAME GREAT, AND YOU WILL BE A BLESSING. I WILL BLESS THOSE WHO BLESS YOU, AND WHOEVER CURSES YOU I WILL CURSE AND ALL PEOPLES ON EARTH WILL BE BLESSED THROUGH YOU."
>
> —GENESIS 12:1–3

And one more thing: You don't have any children. How exactly are your offspring going to be a great nation?

Despite these great odds stacked against them—unable to conceive, seventy-five years old and sixty-five years old, with no idea of where God was leading—Abraham and Sarah showed no signs of a lack of faith. Maybe they were confused and thought God spoke to the wrong people. Perhaps Sarah questioned whether the Lord had indeed spoken to Abraham at all. I can imagine they even briefly argued over the ramifications of God's strange new call on their lives.

But whatever transpired between the lines, Scripture simply says this:

> SO ABRAM WENT, AS THE LORD HAD TOLD HIM. … HE TOOK HIS WIFE SARAI, HIS NEPHEW LOT, ALL THE POSSESSIONS THEY HAD ACCUMULATED AND THE PEOPLE THEY HAD ACQUIRED IN HARRAN, AND THEY SET OUT.
>
> —GENESIS 12:4–5

They packed everything up. They said their final goodbyes. And they set out.

Where did they get this kind of faith? Hebrews 11 gives us the answer:

> FOR HE WAS LOOKING FORWARD TO THE CITY WITH FOUNDATIONS, WHOSE ARCHITECT AND BUILDER IS GOD. AND BY FAITH EVEN SARAH, WHO WAS PAST CHILDBEARING AGE, WAS ENABLED TO BEAR CHILDREN BECAUSE SHE CONSIDERED HIM FAITHFUL WHO HAD MADE THE PROMISE. AND SO FROM THIS ONE MAN, AND HE AS GOOD AS DEAD, CAME DESCENDANTS AS NUMEROUS AS THE STARS IN THE SKY AND AS COUNTLESS AS THE SAND ON THE SEASHORE.
>
> **—HEBREWS 11:10–12**

Looking through their own eyes, they could not see where they were going—much less why they were going. But looking through the eyes of faith, they could see that God was leading them, and that was enough for them.

We'll come back to this story over the next few days, but for now, receive this profound testimony. Seventy-five is not too old. Infertility is not stronger than God. And being "good as dead" is no major obstacle in God's world.

You are not too young or too old. You are not too broken for God to use. You are not worthless or beyond hope. Abraham and Sarah call out to you today, "Keep believing! Don't give up!" ∎

QUESTIONS FOR REFLECTION

CONTENT AND MEANING

READ GENESIS 12:1–5 AND HEBREWS 11:8–12 AGAIN AND ANSWER THE FOLLOWING QUESTIONS.

WHAT STANDS OUT MOST TO YOU FROM THESE TWO PASSAGES ABOUT ABRAHAM AND SARAH'S FAITH?

HEBREWS 11 SAYS THEY LIVED IN TENTS, AS STRANGERS IN A FOREIGN LAND. WHAT OTHER EXAMPLES CAN YOU THINK OF WHEN GOD'S PEOPLE WERE STRANGERS AND EXILES IN FOREIGN LANDS?

WHAT IS "THE CITY WITH FOUNDATIONS," THAT ABRAHAM WAS LOOKING FORWARD TO?

MEDITATION AND APPLICATION

READ GENESIS 12:1–5 AND HEBREWS 11:8–12 AGAIN SLOWLY AND ANSWER THE FOLLOWING QUESTIONS.

WHAT DO YOU THINK WOULD BE THE MOST DIFFICULT OBSTACLE FOR YOU (AGE, INFERTILITY, LACK OF CLARITY) IF YOU WERE IN ABRAHAM AND SARAH'S POSITION?

WHERE IN YOUR LIFE ARE YOU TEMPTED TO THINK THAT YOU ARE "GOOD AS DEAD" IN SOME WAY?

WHAT WOULD IT LOOK LIKE TO LOOK FORWARD TO THE ETERNAL CITY THAT GOD HAS ESTABLISHED FOR ALL HIS PEOPLE? HOW DOES THIS ETERNAL PERSPECTIVE AFFECT THE WAY YOU THINK ABOUT YOUR CURRENT CIRCUMSTANCES?

PRAYER

FINISH YOUR TIME BY PRAYING THAT GOD WOULD GIVE YOU THE PERSPECTIVE TO PRAISE AND TRUST HIM—EVEN IN THE MIDST OF CHALLENGING CIRCUMSTANCES AND UNCLEAR DIRECTIONS.

RISKY FAITH

Yesterday, we read that when God said to go, Abraham packed his things and set out.

Where was God leading him? What was the final destination? And how on earth would a great nation of his offspring bless the nations—when he was seventy-five and his wife was barren?

Abraham didn't know. But still, he got up, trusted God, and began to walk.

WALKING BY FAITH

There's faith, and then there's faith. Risky faith. Bold, against-all-odds faith. *Everyone-will-think-you-are-crazy faith.*

If you're like me, risky faith does not come naturally. Kyle writes:

"We don't like uncertainty; we're taught that it's foolish to walk into the unknown. Therefore we have a tendency to give up if there's no clear map or GPS. But faith that endures has confidence that even when we don't know where we're going, God does. ... Life's detours are undeniably bumpy, confusing, and longer than we anticipate. However, just like actual detours on the road, once we've arrived at our destination, those detours can start to make sense." (28–29)

So Abraham and Sarah set out, not knowing where

they would end up. And for several years, they continued to walk by faith. But they still had no clear destination from God.

Had they misheard him? Had he led them to this nomadic lifestyle without reason? They still didn't have any children, and the families and friends with them were likely becoming increasingly skeptical of this grand plan. But they kept believing and kept walking.

Finally, God spoke again:

"DO NOT BE AFRAID, ABRAM. I AM YOUR SHIELD, YOUR VERY GREAT REWARD."

—GENESIS 15:1

God understood Abraham's confusion. And he even let Abraham question and argue with him. Abraham responded:

"SOVEREIGN LORD, WHAT CAN YOU GIVE ME SINCE I REMAIN CHILDLESS AND THE ONE WHO WILL INHERIT MY ESTATE IS ELIEZER OF DAMASCUS?" AND ABRAM SAID, "YOU HAVE GIVEN ME NO CHILDREN; SO A SERVANT IN MY HOUSEHOLD WILL BE MY HEIR."

—GENESIS 15:2–3

God doubled down on his promises. He affirmed what was spoken years ago, and took Abraham outside and showed him the vast array of glorious stars and planets stretched across the night sky.

FAITH RESTORED

After this encounter with God, the text simply says:

> ABRAM BELIEVED THE LORD, AND [GOD] CREDITED IT TO HIM
> AS RIGHTEOUSNESS.

—GENESIS 15:6

Abraham couldn't see the destination he was traveling to, and he didn't know how he and Sarah fit into the big picture of God's plan for the world. But he kept believing.

If you have ever tried to assemble a large puzzle without the picture of the final project, you know what it's like to have a bunch of pieces and not know what it will produce in the end. Kyle compares this to our ultra-marathon walk of faith. He writes:

"Our faith is in God and the big picture that we won't completely see this side of eternity. It isn't easily—or rarely at all—measured by earthly success, but it's what keeps us aligned with the truth that sings out in our soul. It's faith that keeps believing, even when the pieces don't seem to fit together." (35–36)

DOODLE HERE

CONTENT AND MEANING

READ GENESIS 15:1–6 AGAIN AND ANSWER THE FOLLOWING QUESTIONS.

YEARS PASS BETWEEN THE PROMISE TO ABRAHAM AND ITS FULFILLMENT. WHAT OTHER BIBLICAL EXAMPLES CAN YOU THINK OF WHERE GOD'S PROMISES AND FULFILLMENT ARE STRETCHED ACROSS A LONG PERIOD OF WAITING?

WHY DO YOU THINK GOD SAID, "I AM YOUR SHIELD, YOUR VERY GREAT REWARD." WHY WOULD THIS HAVE BEEN SO ENCOURAGING TO ABRAHAM?

WHAT DOES IT MEAN THAT GOD CREDITED ABRAHAM'S FAITH AS RIGHTEOUSNESS?

MEDITATION AND APPLICATION

READ GENESIS 15:1-6 AGAIN SLOWLY AND ANSWER THE FOLLOWING QUESTIONS.

REFLECTING ON VERSE 1: WHAT DOES IT MEAN TO YOU THAT GOD IS YOUR SHIELD AND YOUR GREAT REWARD? WHAT LESSER DEFENSES OR REWARDS ARE YOU TEMPTED TO TRUST?

WHO IN YOUR LIFE—PRESENT OR PAST—COMES TO MIND WHEN YOU THINK OF RISKY FAITH?

HOW DO YOU FEEL ABOUT ABRAHAM SPEAKING TO GOD OUT OF HIS CONFUSION AND FRUSTRATION? DO YOU FEEL COMFORTABLE TALKING HONESTLY WITH GOD?

DO YOU RESONATE WITH THE IMAGE OF PUTTING TOGETHER A PUZZLE WITHOUT KNOWING WHAT YOU'RE BUILDING? WHAT AREAS OF YOUR LIFE FEEL LIKE THIS AT TIMES?

PRAYER

TAKE A MOMENT TO PRAY TO GOD FOR A BOLD, COURAGEOUS RISKY FAITH TO CONFRONT YOUR FEARS, TRUST HIM, AND KEEP ON WALKING.

REDEFINING FAITH

By faith, Abraham kept walking and kept believing, even when he couldn't see where he was going.

The apostle Paul's letter to the Romans, like Hebrews, calls us to remember the witness of Abraham and Sarah in their walk of risky faith.

AGAINST ALL HOPE, ABRAHAM IN HOPE BELIEVED AND SO BECAME THE FATHER OF MANY NATIONS, JUST AS IT HAD BEEN SAID TO HIM, "SO SHALL YOUR OFFSPRING BE." WITHOUT WEAKENING IN HIS FAITH, HE FACED THE FACT THAT HIS BODY WAS AS GOOD AS DEAD—SINCE HE WAS ABOUT A HUNDRED YEARS OLD—AND THAT SARAH'S WOMB WAS ALSO DEAD. YET HE DID NOT WAVER THROUGH UNBELIEF REGARDING THE PROMISE OF GOD, BUT WAS STRENGTHENED IN HIS FAITH AND GAVE GLORY TO GOD, BEING FULLY PERSUADED THAT GOD HAD POWER TO DO WHAT HE HAD PROMISED.

—ROMANS 4:18–21

Twenty-five years passed after God's initial visit and promise to Abraham. What seemed impossible—Sarah giving birth at age sixty-five—now seemed doubly absurd at age ninety.

And still, Abraham believed. Whatever doubts and reservations he may have had, "he did not waver through unbelief … but was strengthened in his faith." Finally, God's promise became a reality.

AGAINST ALL HOPE, ABRAHAM IN HOPE
BELIEVED AND SO BECAME THE FATHER OF
MANY NATIONS, JUST AS IT HAD BEEN SAID
TO HIM, "SO SHALL YOUR OFFSPRING BE."
WITHOUT WEAKENING IN HIS FAITH, HE FACED
THE FACT THAT HIS BODY WAS AS GOOD
AS DEAD—SINCE HE WAS ABOUT A HUNDRED
YEARS OLD—AND THAT SARAH'S WOMB WAS
ALSO DEAD. YET HE DID NOT WAVER THROUGH
UNBELIEF REGARDING THE PROMISE OF GOD,
BUT WAS STRENGTHENED IN HIS FAITH
AND GAVE GLORY TO GOD, BEING FULLY
PERSUADED THAT GOD HAD POWER TO DO
WHAT HE HAD PROMISED.

—ROMANS 4:18-21

A CHILD IS BORN

In a miracle of miracles, Sarah gave birth to Isaac, and it seemed that all hope was restored. Abraham had a son from which a new people, an entire nation, as numerous as the stars in the sky, could be established. All seemed right among the tents of Abraham and Sarah's people.

That is, until God spoke again.

In Genesis 22, God appeared to Abraham when Isaac is a growing boy and called him to do something unthinkable.

> SOME TIME LATER GOD TESTED ABRAHAM. HE SAID TO HIM, "ABRAHAM!" "HERE I AM," HE REPLIED. THEN GOD SAID, "TAKE YOUR SON, YOUR ONLY SON, WHOM YOU LOVE—ISAAC—AND GO TO THE REGION OF MORIAH. SACRIFICE HIM THERE AS A BURNT OFFERING ON A MOUNTAIN I WILL SHOW YOU."
>
> EARLY THE NEXT MORNING ABRAHAM GOT UP AND LOADED HIS DONKEY. HE TOOK WITH HIM TWO OF HIS SERVANTS AND HIS SON ISAAC. WHEN HE HAD CUT ENOUGH WOOD FOR THE BURNT OFFERING, HE SET OUT FOR THE PLACE GOD HAD TOLD HIM ABOUT. ON THE THIRD DAY ABRAHAM LOOKED UP AND SAW THE PLACE IN THE DISTANCE. HE SAID TO HIS SERVANTS, "STAY HERE WITH THE DONKEY WHILE I AND THE BOY GO OVER THERE. WE WILL WORSHIP AND THEN WE WILL COME BACK TO YOU."
>
> —GENESIS 22:1–5

If this seems like a confusing demand to you, you're not alone. God never requires human sacrifice—indeed, he condemns it in Deuteronomy. And this child, Isaac, was the fulfillment of God's promise made some thirty or forty years before.

And still, Abraham kept believing.

Again God spoke, and again Abraham "set out for the place God had told him about." However, did you catch what he said to his servants?

A FAITH STRONGER THAN DEATH

Abraham told his servants, "Stay here ... and then we will come back." He didn't know how, but he believed Isaac would survive God's test.

Hebrews 11 recounts this as part of Abraham's witness of faith.

> BY FAITH ABRAHAM, WHEN GOD TESTED HIM, OFFERED ISAAC AS A SACRIFICE. HE WHO HAD EMBRACED THE PROMISES WAS ABOUT TO SACRIFICE HIS ONE AND ONLY SON, EVEN THOUGH GOD HAD SAID TO HIM, "IT IS THROUGH ISAAC THAT YOUR OFFSPRING WILL BE RECKONED." ABRAHAM REASONED THAT GOD COULD EVEN RAISE THE DEAD, AND SO IN A MANNER OF SPEAKING HE DID RECEIVE ISAAC BACK FROM DEATH.
>
> **—HEBREWS 11:17–19**

Abraham's faith in God's promise was tested time and time again. But he did not waver. This wasn't a blind faith; he reasoned that God could raise Isaac from the dead.

Abraham knew God; he understood God's promises. With his mind and his heart, he was fully committed to God's ways. There was nothing on earth that could break his faith.

In other words, Abraham had a faith stronger than death.

CONTENT AND MEANING

READ GENESIS 22:1–19, THE ENTIRE NARRATIVE OF ABRAHAM'S TESTING, AND ANSWER THE FOLLOWING QUESTIONS.

WHAT DOES ROMANS 4:18–21 ADD TO THE WITNESS OF ABRAHAM AND SARAH'S FAITH?

WHAT EVIDENCE DO WE HAVE THAT ABRAHAM BELIEVED GOD WOULD NOT LET ISAAC DIE THROUGH THIS EVENT?

WHAT IS THE SIGNIFICANCE OF ABRAHAM'S STATEMENT THAT "GOD HIMSELF WILL PROVIDE THE LAMB" (GENESIS 22:8), WHICH INDEED HAPPENS (VV. 13–14)? HOW DO YOU SEE THIS FORESHADOWING THE OFFERING OF CHRIST'S LIFE ON THE CROSS?

MEDITATION AND APPLICATION

READ ROMANS 4:18-21 AND HEBREWS 11:17-19 SLOWLY AND ANSWER THE FOLLOWING QUESTIONS.

CONSIDER AN INTENSE CHALLENGE, TRIAL, OR TEMPTATION YOU'RE FACING OR HAVE FACED IN LIFE. WHAT WOULD IT LOOK LIKE FOR YOU TO BE STRENGTHENED IN YOUR FAITH, GIVE GLORY TO GOD, AND BE FULLY PERSUADED THAT GOD HAS THE POWER TO DO WHAT HE HAS PROMISED (ROMANS 4:21)?

WHERE DO YOU FEEL LIKE GOD IS ASKING YOU TO BELIEVE THE IMPOSSIBLE OR DO WHAT SEEMS UNBEARABLE?

CONSIDER THE PARALLELS TO GOD'S OFFERING OF HIS OWN FIRST AND ONLY SON. HOW ARE YOU ENCOURAGED THAT, IN CHRIST, GOD HIMSELF HAS PROVIDED A LAMB FOR THE SACRIFICE (GENESIS 22:8)?

PRAYER

TAKE A MOMENT TO POUR OUT YOUR THANKS TO GOD FOR HIS SENDING HIS ONLY SON TO LIVE AND DIE AND BE RAISED TO LIFE—ALL FOR US. PRAISE GOD FOR HIS GLORY AND WISDOM AND POWER IN ACHIEVING OUR SALVATION, FULFILLING HIS PROMISES, AND WAKING US TO NEW ETERNAL LIFE.

THE TRUE AND BETTER ABRAHAM

In the darkest of situations, in the most unlikely moments, and against all the odds, Abraham believed in God and his promises. Abraham stands as chief among a crowd of witnesses urging us to: Keep going! Keep walking! Keep believing! He is our witness to an unwavering faith in what he could not see and an unshakeable hope in the glory that awaited him for all eternity.

And yet, there is one even greater than Abraham.

ABRAHAM'S DESCENDANT

John 8 tells the story of a long dispute between Jesus and the Pharisees. The Pharisees were looking for a way to trap Jesus in his words and catch him in an error they could use against him. And yet at every accusation, Jesus responded with restraint, wisdom, and clarity about who he is, and how they are the ones in error.

Finally, the dispute reached a climax: "Abraham is our father," the Pharisees said, defending their standing as God's people through their ancestor's faith. "If you were Abraham's children," Jesus responded to the angry crowd of religious leaders, "then you would do what Abraham did" (John 8:39).

Taking things one step further, Jesus stated, "Abraham rejoiced at the thought of seeing my day; he saw it and was glad. ... Very truly I tell you, before Abraham was born, I Am!" (John 8:56, 58).

What was Jesus referring to? According to Matthew 1, Jesus was a direct offspring of Abraham. From Isaac came Jacob, from Jacob came Judah, and on down the line, through David and Solomon, down to a man named Joseph, the husband of Mary, the woman who gave birth to Jesus, who is called Messiah (Matthew 1:16).

In every sense, Jesus was Abraham's true son, but it goes even further than that.

Jesus said that he existed before Abraham and that Abraham rejoiced at the thought of his day. In other words, Jesus is the true and better Abraham.

• Jesus is the true and better Son of God who perfectly obeyed his Father.
• Jesus is the true and better one to lead his people toward the holy land of God.
• Jesus is the true and better sacrifice, the only Son who was offered in place of you and me.
• Jesus is the true and better Abraham, who died in glory—but didn't stay dead, and now reigns over creation and intercedes on our behalf.

Abraham stands in the heavenly places as a witness to God's power and faithfulness. He shouts, "Keep believing!" and he points us to the One that he foreshadowed. The true and better Abraham, Jesus Christ the Messiah.

ABRAHAM STANDS AS

CHIEF AMONG A CROWD

OF WITNESSES URGING

US TO: KEEP GOING! KEEP

WALKING! KEEP BELIEVING!

CONTENT AND MEANING

READ JOHN 8:31–59, JESUS' DIALOGUE WITH THE PHARISEES OVER ABRAHAM, AND ANSWER THE FOLLOWING QUESTIONS.

IN WHAT WAYS IS JESUS THE TRUE AND BETTER ABRAHAM?

WHY DID THE PHARISEES BECOME SO UPSET ABOUT JESUS' STATEMENTS ABOUT ABRAHAM?

WHAT ARE THE MOST IMPORTANT THINGS YOU LEARNED THIS WEEK ABOUT ABRAHAM AND SARAH AND THEIR WITNESS OF FAITH?

MEDITATION AND APPLICATION

READ HEBREWS 11:8–19 SLOWLY AND ANSWER THE FOLLOWING QUESTIONS.

REFLECTING ON THE WHOLE STORY OF ABRAHAM AND SARAH, IN WHAT AREAS DO YOU RESONATE WITH THEIR WITNESS?

• CALLED TO LEAVE FAMILY AND HOME IN OBEDIENCE TO GOD

• ASKED TO FOLLOW GOD INTO AN UNKNOWN PLACE OR SITUATION

• MADE TO WAIT FOR YEARS (EVEN DECADES) FOR THE FULFILLMENT OF A PROMISE

• LIVING AS A FOREIGNER OR STRANGER IN A DISTANT LAND

• ASKED TO GIVE UP SOMETHING VERY DEAR

WHAT ARE SOME PRACTICAL WAYS YOU CAN LIVE IN FAITH AND OBEDIENCE TO GOD AS A RESULT OF THIS REFLECTION ON THE LIFE AND WITNESS OF ABRAHAM AND SARAH?

PRAYER

PRAY TO THE FATHER THAT HE WOULD GIVE YOU THE FAITH AND RESOLVE OF ABRAHAM AND SARAH AS YOU LOOK TO CHRIST. PRAISE HIM FOR HIS FAITHFULNESS AND PLEDGE YOUR FAITH IN HIS PROMISES AGAIN.

REFLECTION AND REVIEW

O n the seventh day of each week, we're going to pause to review and reflect on the past week. If you are behind a day or two, use this day to catch up. If you are caught up, use this day to review the previous six days' notes, especially all the Scripture references and stories. Use these seventh days to review your responses and prayers as well.

TAKE A MARKER   TRACE OVER THE LETTERS

therefore SINCE WE ARE SURROUNDED by such a great CLOUD OF WITNESSES LET US THROW OFF HINDERS everything THAT SO EASILY SIN ENTANGLES & LET US run WITH perseverance THE RACE marked OUT FOR US

QUESTIONS FOR REFLECTION

BASED ON YOUR WEEK'S READING AND
REFLECTION, READ THIS VERSE AGAIN AND
ANSWER THE FOLLOWING QUESTIONS.

"SINCE WE ARE SURROUNDED BY SUCH A GREAT
CLOUD OF WITNESSES, LET US THROW OFF
EVERYTHING THAT HINDERS AND ... RUN WITH
PERSEVERANCE THE RACE MARKED OUT FOR
US."

—HEBREWS 12:1

WHAT WERE THE MOST SIGNIFICANT THINGS
YOU LEARNED ABOUT GOD'S FAITHFULNESS
AND THE CHRISTIAN LIFE THIS WEEK?

WHAT WAS THE MOST SIGNIFICANT THING YOU
LEARNED ABOUT THE "ULTRA-MARATHON" OF
FAITH THIS WEEK?

WHAT WAS THE MOST SIGNIFICANT
THING YOU LEARNED ABOUT YOURSELF
THIS WEEK? WHERE DO YOU SENSE GOD
INVITING YOU INTO DEEPER FAITH AND
TRUST IN HIM?

WHAT WOULD YOUR LIFE LOOK LIKE IF
YOU FULLY BELIEVED AND LIVED LIKE
ABRAHAM'S WITNESS TO KEEP BELIEVING
THIS WEEK?

TWO

HALL OF FAME

THESE WERE ALL COMMENDED
FOR THEIR FAITH, YET NONE OF THEM
RECEIVED WHAT HAD BEEN PROMISED.

—HEBREWS 11:39

DESPERATE MOMENTS

Don't give up.

That's the message. This life will challenge, try, and confront us over and over again. The Christian life is not free from hardship and suffering. On the contrary, life in Christ is full of all the demands that the rest of the world faces, and all of the challenges and trials of spiritual and church life.

What we need is real encouragement—a battle cry, a call to action, marching orders to push back the darkness. We need to stand and face our fears and enemies, and remember that we are not alone.

But where do we find such encouragement in a marathon-long life of faith and endurance?

THE HALL OF FAITH

Hebrews 12 begins with this statement:

THEREFORE, SINCE WE ARE
SURROUNDED BY SUCH A

GREAT CLOUD OF
WITNESSES, LET
US THROW OFF
EVERYTHING THAT
HINDERS AND THE
SIN THAT SO EASILY
ENTANGLES. AND
LET US RUN WITH
PERSEVERANCE THE
RACE MARKED OUT FOR
US, FIXING OUR EYES
ON JESUS, THE PIONEER
AND PERFECTER OF
FAITH.
—HEBREWS 12:1–2

In context (remember the transition word "Therefore"), Hebrews 12 encourages based on the truths of Hebrews 11. And Hebrews 11 is a famous chapter we often call the Hall of Faith. In it, the author reminds us of the faith and endurance of o forefathers and spiritual mothers.

Noah—who built an ark in faith of God's words alone
Abraham and Sarah—who left home and family to follow God to an unknown place
Jacob—who tried to run from his problems and found himself wrestling with God
Moses—who refused to let Israel be oppressed and led God's people to the promised land
Joshua—who simply walked in faith until the walls of God's enemies fell in a heap
Gideon—whose little army was empowered by an all-powerful God
Nehemiah—who worked day and night to rebuild Jerusalem while surrounded by doubters
Paul—who finished the race, kept the faith, and passed on to us the charge to build the church

These were all witnesses of God's power and goodness to his people in the unlikeliest of scenarios. They all were pressed to their limits, hit the wall of desperation, and had to fight back the temptation to give up.

They all faced their own desperate moments. And as a result, they experienced God's deliverance in historic ways.

DESPERATE MOMENTS

Kyle Idleman, in *Don't Give Up*, writes this:

"There is something about a desperate moment—a cold, pitch-black moment when all hope seems lost—that causes us to call out God's name in distress. In that moment of desperation, when you feel like things are out of your control and there is nothing you can do, there is a profound opportunity."(43)

When was the last time you faced a moment of complete desperation? I don't mean binging a Netflix show and not being able to find something new. I mean *real desperation*. You have tried everything to get through to your teenager, and he won't even look at you. You just received a grim cancer diagnosis. Your mother has passed away and you can't imagine life without her. You lost your job and bills are piled a foot high on the kitchen counter. *What now?*

These desperate moments feel like the lowest points of life. But could they often be gifts from a good and loving God?

"The point of defeat—the urge to throw up your hands and surrender—seems like the most desolate corner of creation. It actually places you in prime position to experience God's strength and provision because, as it turns out, God is drawn to the desperate. If you trace this idea in Scripture, you'll find that God's deliverance often follows closely upon a time of desperation. His blessing tends to fall upon a condition of brokenness. Throughout history, his most powerful servants have all come from a place of desolation and defeat." (Idleman 43)

In these desperate moments, we need to turn back to the Scriptures. And I don't mean for "everything will work out" platitudes. We need the dark, gritty, brutally honest tales of women and men who lost it all and cried out to God.

We need folks who have wrestled with God and come away with a limp. In short, we need the Hall of Fame.

CONTENT AND MEANING

CONSIDER HEBREWS 12:1–2 AND THE EXAMPLES OF FAITH LISTED ABOVE.

WHAT DO THE HEROES OF THE FAITH IN THE OLD AND NEW TESTAMENTS HAVE IN COMMON? WHAT CONSISTENCIES LIE IN THEIR STORIES?

THINKING BACK TO LAST WEEK, WHAT WERE SOME OF THE DESPERATE MOMENTS THAT ABRAHAM AND SARAH FACED? HOW DID THEY RESPOND?

HOW DOES HEBREWS 12:1–2 FOCUS THE WALK OF FAITH IN TIMES OF TOTAL DESPERATION?

MEDITATION AND APPLICATION

REFLECT ON THE MOST SIGNIFICANT CHALLENGES
YOU'RE FACING RIGHT NOW. WRITE OUT ONE SITUATION
OR RELATIONSHIP THAT HAS BROUGHT YOU TO THE
END OF YOURSELF.

WHAT PROMISES OF GOD COME TO MIND? WHICH
EXAMPLES IN THE SCRIPTURES ALIGN MOST CLOSELY
WITH YOUR TIME OF NEED?

HOW DO YOU THINK THE HALL OF FAITH CAN GIVE YOU
FRESH ENCOURAGEMENT IN THIS CHALLENGE?

PRAYER

PRAY TODAY, ASKING THE GOD OF COMFORT TO GIVE YOU FRESH
COURAGE AND COMFORT FOR YOUR DESPERATION. BRING WITH
UTTER HONESTY YOUR CHALLENGES BEFORE HIM, AND COMMIT
YOUR WAYS TO HIM.

KEEP FIGHTING: THE WITNESS OF JACOB

Yesterday, we said that we need real encouragement for the long endurance walk of faith. We need the stories of Old and New Testament witnesses who have walked with God, cried out to God, and even wrestled with God.

We need the story of Jacob.

SIBLING RIVALRY

Jacob was the son of Isaac—the son of Abraham, who we met briefly last week. All three are mentioned in the Hall of Fame of Hebrews 11, and all three were the founders of the Hebrew faith and community. But it wasn't always so straightforward for Jacob.

Jacob and his twin brother, Esau, had a sibling rivalry for the ages. I have three sons, and they play and fight and compete constantly. But Jacob and Esau were on another level. Their rivalry lasted decades and spanned countries in pursuit of one another.

Esau was a man's man. He loved the outdoors, was strong and motivated, and was proficient in hunting. Jacob, on the other hand, appears to have been quiet and gentle, and enjoyed the finer things in life; he hung by his mother's side and enjoyed baking.

By all worldly accounts, Esau was the chosen son. He was the firstborn, the rightful heir, the strong protector, and provider of the family. And Jacob was his scrawny, shifty, jealous younger (by half a minute) brother.

Early in adult life, Esau had been out hunting for days while Jacob remained home cooking, and Esau came in hungry. Not just hungry though—famished, starving. He was "hangry." And Jacob, whose name means "deceiver," saw an opportunity. Esau begged Jacob for food, and Jacob said, "First, sell me your birthright" (Genesis 25:31). Esau quickly pledged it to him and began to eat. And just like that, in a culture of binding contracts, Jacob seized the place of firstborn and heir in the family.

Later in life, when Isaac was on his deathbed, the old patriarch sent out Esau to hunt and prepare one last great meal for him. While Esau was away, Jacob worked with his mother to trick Isaac. Jacob dressed up as Esau and took advantage of his father's advanced age and poor vision. Jacob stole the blessing that Isaac intended for Esau (Genesis 27). Once again, Jacob snuck away with the upper hand—much to Esau's unrelenting anger.

Fearing Esau's wrath and strength, Jacob fled. And that's when he realized his mistake. He couldn't return home. He couldn't enjoy his birthright. He was a fugitive, alone and on the run. Jacob would spend years looking over his shoulder, scanning the hills, forever fearful that Esau might appear with a band of warriors to take his life.

His life became one of desperation and fear.

When we find ourselves in a situation where we don't think we have what it takes, we run away. The problem is that fear distorts our perception of reality. It tells us late at night that the jacket strewn over the chair is some kind of monster or intruder.

Fear convinces us to give up before we've even tried. This is what giving up may look like:

Running away before the race has even started.
Running from friendship to friendship.
Running from conflict to conflict.
Running from broken promise to broken promise.

"Fear causes most of us to run away. That's what Jacob did. That was his pattern until finally there was nowhere to run. That's one potential that always becomes real: the place where there's nowhere else to run."(Idleman 51)

Perhaps you can identify with this fear. You've made a mess of your life. You've left behind those who could help you. And now there's no turning back. You're stuck between a rock and a hard place.

But before you quit, before you run away, you need to look to the crowd. See the witness of Jacob and keep fighting!

_____

DOODLE HERE

CONTENT AND MEANING

TAKE A FEW MINUTES TO READ GENESIS 25-27 AND ANSWER THE FOLLOWING QUESTIONS.

WHAT HEAVY BURDENS COULD HAVE BEEN PLACED ON JACOB BY HIS FAMILY OF ORIGIN? WHY DO YOU THINK THE SIBLING RIVALRY WITH ESAU WAS SO INTENSE?

WHY DID JACOB WANT TO STEAL ESAU'S BIRTHRIGHT? WHY DO YOU THINK ESAU WAS WILLING TO GIVE IT TO HIM?

GIVEN WHAT YOU KNOW ABOUT JACOB AT THIS POINT IN THE STORY, WHY DO YOU THINK HE IS INCLUDED IN HEBREWS 11'S HALL OF FAME?

QUESTIONS FOR REFLECTION

MEDITATION AND APPLICATION

REFLECT DEEPLY ON THE FOLLOWING QUESTIONS.

IN WHAT WAYS DO YOU RESONATE WITH ESAU?
WHAT ABOUT JACOB?

WHERE IN YOUR LIFE DO YOU FIND YOURSELF
"RUNNING AWAY" IN FEAR? WHERE DO YOU FEEL
FEAR FOR A "FUTURE STORY THAT HASN'T BEEN
WRITTEN YET"?

PRAYER
WHATEVER BURDENS, FEARS, OR TRIALS YOU ARE CARRYING,
PRAY THAT THE LORD WOULD LIFT THEM NOW. AS 1 PETER 5:7
SAYS, "CAST ALL YOUR ANXIETY ON HIM BECAUSE HE CARES
FOR YOU." PRAY TO THE FATHER FOR INCREASED FAITH AND
PEACE IN YOUR WALK WITH HIM.

WRESTLING WITH GOD

W hen facing intense challenges, we all experience "fight or flight."

Sometimes we are going to fight back when wisdom tells us to walk away. Other times we may run from situations that require a good hard battle.

In Genesis 25–27, we see Jacob consistently chose "flight." He ran from his problems, and then ran from the problems that those problems created. As a result, he became a fugitive, doing life on the lam.

After spending time with his family member Laban, Jacob had to flee again. The only place he could safely go was toward home—but that was back into Esau's territory.

NOWHERE LEFT TO RUN

Jacob hadn't seen Esau since cheating him out of his birthright, so he sent messengers ahead with a gift and a peaceful greeting. The response came back: Esau was coming, and he was bringing four hundred men with him.

At this point, Jacob must have been thinking, when did Esau build an army? I'm dead meat.

Jacob split his family into two groups, assuming only one group would be defeated so the other would be spared, and then he hid by himself. Crying out to the Lord, Jacob prayed:

"O GOD OF MY FATHER ABRAHAM, GOD OF MY FATHER ISAAC, LORD, YOU WHO SAID TO ME, 'GO BACK TO YOUR COUNTRY AND YOUR RELATIVES, AND I WILL MAKE YOU PROSPER,' I AM UNWORTHY OF ALL THE KINDNESS AND

FAITHFULNESS YOU HAVE SHOWN YOUR SERVANT. I HAD ONLY
MY STAFF WHEN I CROSSED THIS JORDAN, BUT NOW I HAVE
BECOME TWO CAMPS. SAVE ME, I PRAY, FROM THE HAND OF MY
BROTHER ESAU, FOR I AM AFRAID HE WILL COME AND ATTACK
ME, AND ALSO THE MOTHERS WITH THEIR CHILDREN. BUT YOU
HAVE SAID, 'I WILL SURELY MAKE YOU PROSPER AND WILL
MAKE YOUR DESCENDANTS LIKE THE SAND OF THE SEA, WHICH
CANNOT BE COUNTED.'"

—GENESIS 32:9–12

This is the first time we see Jacob cry out before the Lord. Finally, he had nowhere left to run. He had come to the end of himself. He must depend on God alone.

RUMBLE IN THE JUNGLE

That night, as Jacob was alone, he was confronted by a strong warrior. Jacob must have been thinking, Esau has found me, and now he wants to kill me. The text says, "a man wrestled with him till daybreak" (Genesis 32:24).

Jacob put up a strong fight throughout the night, and when the man saw that he could not defeat Jacob, he "touched the socket of Jacob's hip so that his hip was wrenched" and said, "Let me go, for it is daybreak" (Genesis 32:25–26). In the moment, Jacob appeared to have won the fight—though his hip was dislocated.

So Jacob, who still needed his brother's affirmation and blessing so that he wouldn't have to spend his life on the run, made a demand:

JACOB REPLIED, "I WILL NOT LET YOU GO UNLESS YOU BLESS ME." THE MAN ASKED HIM, "WHAT IS YOUR NAME?" "JACOB," HE ANSWERED. THEN THE MAN SAID, "YOUR NAME WILL NO LONGER BE JACOB, BUT ISRAEL, BECAUSE YOU HAVE STRUGGLED WITH GOD AND WITH HUMANS AND HAVE OVERCOME." JACOB SAID, "PLEASE TELL ME YOUR NAME." BUT HE REPLIED, "WHY DO YOU ASK MY NAME?" THEN HE BLESSED HIM THERE. SO JACOB CALLED THE PLACE PENIEL, SAYING, "IT IS BECAUSE I SAW GOD FACE TO FACE, AND YET MY LIFE WAS SPARED."

—GENESIS 32:26–30

Like a shocking plot twist in a great movie, we suddenly realize that Jacob had been wrestling with God.

"Jacob has been wrestling with God. He faced the fight he has avoided all his life. Like Jonah, like so many others in the Scriptures and in our lives, his lesson is that you can't run away from God.

But something has changed in Jacob. Once it's on, once he's wrestling, he won't stop until he gets a blessing out of it. This is the moment he goes from being Gypping Jacob to Chosen Israel. This is where the scheming, the fear, and the flight come to an end and the blessings begin.

Every good thing is possible. But not without a fight." (Idleman 53)

YOU CAN'T RUN FOREVER. SOMETIMES YOU NEED TO STAY AND FIGHT. SOMETIMES YOU HAVE TO WRESTLE WITH GOD UNTIL YOU GET THE BLESSING. KEEP FIGHTING!

CONTENT AND MEANING

READ GENESIS 32 AND ANSWER THE FOLLOWING QUESTIONS.

WHY COULD JACOB NOT REMAIN IN LABAN'S LAND? HOW DID HE BECOME A MAN WITHOUT A HOME?

WHY WAS JACOB SO AFRAID OF MEETING ESAU ALONG THE WAY?

JACOB HAD BEEN GIVEN THE PROMISE THAT, LIKE ABRAHAM, HIS OFFSPRING WOULD BE NUMEROUS AND SIGNIFICANT (GENESIS 32:12). HOW DOES THIS PROMISE CHANGE THE WAY JACOB PRAYS?

MEDITATION AND APPLICATION

REFLECT DEEPLY ON THE FOLLOWING QUESTIONS.

WHAT PROMISES OF GOD—WHETHER FROM
SCRIPTURE FOR ALL GOD'S PEOPLE OR PERSONAL
TO YOU—CAN YOU CLING TO WHEN YOU REACH
DESPERATE PLACES?

WHERE IN YOUR LIFE DO YOU THINK GOD IS
CALLING YOU TO NOT RUN, BUT HOLD GROUND
AND FIGHT?

IN WHAT WAYS DO YOU, LIKE JACOB, WALK WITH
A LIMP? HOW HAS SOME FORM OF SUFFERING
OR STRUGGLE CHANGED THE WAY YOU MOVE
THROUGH LIFE UNDER THE PROMISES OF GOD?

PRAYER

PRAY THAT GOD WOULD BECOME MORE REAL TO YOU THAN
EVER BEFORE. WHATEVER FEARS OR BURDENS YOU HAVE,
WRESTLE WITH GOD IN PRAYER THAT HE WOULD GIVE YOU
FREEDOM FROM THEM. JUST AS JACOB WAS RENAMED
ISRAEL, THANK GOD THAT HE HAS SAVED YOU AND CALLED
YOU HIS OWN SON OR DAUGHTER.

KEEP PERSPECTIVE

In 2010, thirty-three miners were trapped underground in Chile for more than two months.

The story is told in a book called *Deep Down Dark*. For the miners, survival underground was impossible. Their chances of rescue were slim to none. So in their desperation, they began to take stock of their lives and ask deep questions.

Many turned to God for the first time. They began to pray, confess their sins, and trust God with their dramatic need.

No one wants to be in the deep-down dark, but that's often where God does his best work.

ORDINARY HEROES

This was Jacob's situation. When he could run no more, when he was finally alone, he had to face the darkness. Jacob believed in God before this wrestling match. But now God was real. After decades of empty scheming and fearful running, Jacob finally became silent and still. Now God showed up in a powerful way.

Kyle puts it this way:

"God doesn't want to leave you like you were before the addiction, or abuse, or affair, or relationship, or financial devastation, or diagnosis, or failure. He wants to bless you and introduce you to a whole new world of meaning and opportunity. But sometimes you have to fight through the night to get to the blessing." (56)

Jacob doesn't seem like a traditional Bible hero. He lacks Abraham's faith, Moses's resolve, and David's passion. In fact, he seems pretty ordinary.

Indeed, the Bible is full of ordinary heroes—and that's not a contradiction.

Hebrews 11 describes an entire part of the crowd of witnesses that don't even get mentioned by name.

WOMEN RECEIVED BACK THEIR DEAD, RAISED TO LIFE AGAIN. THERE WERE OTHERS WHO WERE TORTURED, REFUSING TO BE RELEASED SO THAT THEY MIGHT GAIN AN EVEN BETTER RESURRECTION. SOME FACED JEERS AND FLOGGING, AND EVEN CHAINS AND IMPRISONMENT. THEY WERE PUT TO DEATH BY STONING; THEY WERE SAWED IN TWO; THEY WERE KILLED BY THE SWORD. THEY WENT ABOUT IN SHEEPSKINS AND GOATSKINS, DESTITUTE, PERSECUTED AND MISTREATED— THE WORLD WAS NOT WORTHY OF THEM. THEY WANDERED IN DESERTS AND MOUNTAINS, LIVING IN CAVES AND IN HOLES IN THE GROUND.

—HEBREWS 11:35–38

We probably have more in common with these unnamed heroes than we do with Moses and David. Through their intense persecution, they serve as a model of faithfulness.

"They carried out lives of obscure greatness. One message these unnamed witnesses might have for us is to keep perspective the next time we're struggling with discouragement.

The next time you feel like your situation isn't fair and you're ready to give up, remember those who faced jeers and flogging, chains and imprisonment." (Idleman 63)

ORDINARY HEROES

These witnesses are calling out, "Don't give up! Keep believing, keep fighting, keep perspective!"

We all—like Jacob and these unnamed heroes—face strong resistance and discouragement. We live in a world that's often hostile to our faith.

These witnesses remind us that we are not alone. Even if you are the only believer in your family, you are not alone. You might be the only Christian at work, but you are not alone. Maybe nobody understands your quiet suffering, but you are not alone.

The witnesses of Hebrews 11 encourage you to keep this global, eternal perspective. No doubt, your pain and suffering are real. It is right to feel overwhelmed.

But don't give up. You are not alone, and God will provide the strength for today's challenges. Keep going!

QUESTIONS FOR REFLECTION

CONTENT AND MEANING

READ HEBREWS 11:35-38 AND ANSWER THE FOLLOWING QUESTIONS.

WHY DO YOU THINK THE AUTHOR OF HEBREWS INCLUDES THESE OTHER UNNAMED EXAMPLES OF FAITH ALONG WITH THE WELL-KNOWN WOMEN AND MEN OF THE SCRIPTURES?

WHY DOES IT SAY THAT THE WORLD WAS NOT WORTHY OF THESE INDIVIDUALS?

MEDITATION AND APPLICATION

READ HEBREWS 11:35–38 AGAIN SLOWLY AND REFLECT ON THE FOLLOWING QUESTIONS.

WHERE IN YOUR LIFE ARE YOU FACING SOME FORM OF PERSECUTION?

IN WHAT RELATIONSHIPS DO YOU FEEL DISCOURAGED, DESPERATE, OR EXHAUSTED? HOW DO THE EXAMPLES OF GREAT FAITH IN EXTRAORDINARY CHALLENGES ENCOURAGE YOU TO KEEP GOING?

WHAT IS YOUR ONE BIG TAKEAWAY FROM THE LIFE OF JACOB? WHAT DO YOU WANT TO REMEMBER FROM HIS "WITNESS"?

PRAYER

PRAY FOR MORE FAITH IN ENDURING TRIALS AND PERSECUTIONS AMONG NON-BELIEVERS. PRAY FOR FAITH TO ENTER SITUATIONS OF INCREASED APATHY AND HOSTILITY FOR THE SAKE OF GOD'S GLORY. PRAY FOR THOSE WHO ARE FACING HARDSHIP AND PERSECUTION IN THEIR OWN LIVES.

CHANGE YOUR PERSPECTIVE

L ife is hard, trials are constant, and suffering surrounds us. However, there are some ways that we make things harder and more hopeless than they need to be. If we view ourselves as a victim of our circumstances, we'll never find the encouragement we need for the long walk of faith and endurance.

LOSE THE VICTIM MENTALITY

Even if you think, I don't have a victim mentality, don't skip this part just yet. As Kyle writes, "A victim mentality can be hard to self-diagnose because it's not always pervasive" (65). We often take the role of victim in one or two areas in life. Often these are areas where we're tempted to give up. To be able to recognize where you may have adopted a victimized viewpoint can help you find the perspective to endure.

Consider the following statements and questions.

People with a victim mentality tend to whine and complain. Do you feel underpaid and unappreciated at work? Do you ever complain about how others treat you?

People with a victim mentality tend to blame and criticize. Do you ever try to defend yourself when someone suggests you may be responsible for an error or oversight? Are you often critical of your church, company, or social gatherings?

People with a victim mentality tend to compare and covet. Do you notice what others are wearing or driving and feel that you deserve better than what you have?

People with a victim mentality tend to be cynical and pessimistic. Do you find yourself giving up on a diet or workout plan, or moving away from a friend group because it seems like too much work?

You may not have a victim mentality in all of life, but if there's an area of your life where you're experiencing self-pity, you may be likely to give up there.

CHANGE YOUR PERSPECTIVE

As Kyle writes, "I know that for me, choosing not to feel sorry for myself comes much easier when I get a little dose of true perspective" (68). Consider a few quick examples of recent real-life witnesses of enduring faith.

John Wesley, born in 1703, was the fifteenth child in his family and grew up poor. He became one of the greatest preachers in American history, often speaking to tens of thousands of people in public spaces.

William Carey was one of the first missionaries to India, and lost his wife and child on the mission field. He kept up the work, and today hundreds of churches in India trace their roots back to his work.

Adoniram Judson was a missionary to Burma, but his first wife and three children died, and later his second wife and two children also died there. Still he persisted, and in the end he had led more than six thousand people to Christ and planted more than sixty churches.

According to Acts 14:22, "We must go through many hardships to enter the kingdom of God." If you expect resistance and hardship, if you are ready for trials and temptations, and if you lose the victim mentality, you can profoundly change your perspective.

As Romans 12:2 says, "Do not conform to the pattern of this world, but be transformed by the renewing of your mind." We renew our minds by focusing on Christ, listening to the witnesses who have gone before us, and enduring the trials intended to make us holy and wise.

"DO NOT CONFORM
TO THE PATTERN OF
THIS WORLD, BUT BE
TRANSFORMED BY THE
RENEWING OF YOUR
MIND."

CONTENT AND MEANING

READ HEBREWS 11:35-38 AGAIN AND ANSWER THE FOLLOWING QUESTIONS.

HOW DO THE EXAMPLES OF THE THREE MISSIONARIES DISCUSSED DEMONSTRATE THE TRUTHS OF HEBREWS 11:35-38?

READ ROMANS 12:1-2. WHAT DOES IT MEAN TO GIVE YOUR LIFE AS A LIVING SACRIFICE? HOW DO YOU BECOME TRANSFORMED BY THE RENEWAL OF YOUR MIND?

THINK BACK TO THE LIFE AND WITNESS OF JACOB. HOW DOES HIS LIFE DEMONSTRATE A PATTERN OF HARDSHIP AND SUFFERING FOLLOWED BY MATURITY AND GODLINESS?

QUESTIONS FOR REFLECTION

MEDITATION AND APPLICATION

REFLECT ON THE FOLLOWING QUESTIONS.

WHEN YOU READ, "WE MUST GO THROUGH MANY HARDSHIPS TO ENTER THE KINGDOM OF GOD" (ACTS 14:22), HOW DOES IT MAKE YOU FEEL? HOW HAVE YOU SEEN THIS TO BE TRUE?

CONSIDER THE FOUR EXAMPLES OF A VICTIM MENTALITY LISTED IN THIS DAY'S CONTENT. WHICH DO YOU FEEL MAY BE TRUE OF YOU?

IF YOU HAD THE FAITH AND ENDURANCE OF THE GREAT MISSIONARIES, WHAT DO YOU THINK THE OUTCOME OF YOUR LIFE WOULD BE?

PRAYER

THANK GOD FOR ENABLING THE RENEWAL OF YOUR MIND IN CHRIST. ASK HIM TO SHOW YOU WHERE SELF-PITY HAS ROBBED YOU OF PEACE AND JOY. PRAY THAT GOD WOULD GRANT YOU THE ABILITY TO SUFFER WELL FOR HIM AND, THROUGH YOUR SUFFERING, BRING OTHERS TO CHRIST.

CHOOSE GRATITUDE

We began this week with a simple message: Don't give up.

This life will challenge and try and confront us over and over. The Christian life is not free from hardship and suffering. What we need, then, is real encouragement—a battle cry, a call to action, marching orders to push back darkness. We need to stand and face our fears and enemies, remembering that we are not alone.

There's one more way we can find true encouragement for the marathon-long life of faith and endurance. We can *choose gratitude*.

TALK TO YOURSELF

Have you ever noticed that the Bible tells you to talk to yourself?

It may seem odd, but it's true. In Psalms 42–43, the psalmist repeats this refrain over and over:

PUT YOUR HOPE IN GOD, FOR I WILL YET PRAISE HIM.

—PSALM 42:5, 11; 43:5

The question is not whether you engage in self-talk, but what you're saying to yourself. What would happen if you said these things to yourself numerous times each day: "You're no good. You're going to blow it again. You always mess things up. No one likes you. They've all gotten together and decided that you're out." What would happen? You would begin to believe those words and your day would be ruined.

But what would happen if you said this instead: "I am a child of God. My sins are forgiven. I'm far from perfect, but God loves me as I am. He has given me purpose. He has gifted me to serve others. I can make it through many challenges." You would begin to believe those words and your day would be full of power and energy.

In a closing appeal to his followers, the apostle Paul wrote these words of encouragement:

REJOICE IN THE LORD ALWAYS. I WILL SAY IT AGAIN: REJOICE! LET YOUR GENTLENESS BE EVIDENT TO ALL. THE LORD IS NEAR. DO NOT BE ANXIOUS ABOUT ANYTHING, BUT IN EVERY SITUATION, BY PRAYER AND PETITION, WITH THANKSGIVING, PRESENT YOUR REQUESTS TO GOD. AND THE PEACE OF GOD, WHICH TRANSCENDS ALL UNDERSTANDING, WILL GUARD YOUR HEARTS AND YOUR MINDS IN CHRIST JESUS. FINALLY, BROTHERS AND SISTERS, WHATEVER IS TRUE, WHATEVER IS NOBLE, WHATEVER IS RIGHT, WHATEVER IS PURE, WHATEVER IS LOVELY, WHATEVER IS ADMIRABLE—IF ANYTHING IS EXCELLENT OR PRAISEWORTHY—THINK ABOUT SUCH THINGS.

—PHILIPPIANS 4:4–8

THINK ABOUT SUCH THINGS

Paul is giving you powerful encouragement—putting courage in you—with these words. Take them to heart! When you feel tired and discouraged, when you are tempted to listen to the broken record of condemnation, remember these words: Rejoice! Present your requests to God. His peace will guard your heart and mind in Christ.

When we change our thinking, when we think about such things as these—whatever is true, noble, right, pure, lovely, admirable, excellent, and praiseworthy—our minds become re-oriented around what God has done for us. We remember that he is good, his love endures forever, and his faithfulness lasts through all generations (see Psalm 107).

In other words, when you feel like giving up, talk to yourself! Speak words of truth. Remember and rehearse the words of Scripture. Pray that God would cover you with his transcendent peace. Set your mind on things above!

When you choose gratitude and present your requests to God, you find encouragement for the long walk of faith.

QUESTIONS FOR REFLECTION

CONTENT AND MEANING

READ PHILIPPIANS 4:4-8 AND ANSWER THE FOLLOWING QUESTIONS.

WHY DOES PAUL SAY TO "REJOICE IN THE LORD ALWAYS."? WHY WOULD GOD CALL HIS PEOPLE TO FIND JOY (REJOICE) EVEN WHEN WE DON'T FEEL JOYFUL?

WHAT DOES THE PROMISE "THE LORD IS NEAR." IMPLY? HOW DOES THE NEARNESS OF GOD EMPOWER US?

THINKING BACK TO THE LIVES OF ABRAHAM AND JACOB, HOW HAVE YOU SEEN THESE EXAMPLES CHOOSE GRATITUDE WHEN SELF-PITY COULD HAVE BEEN CHOSEN?

MEDITATION AND APPLICATION

READ PHILIPPIANS 4:4-8 AGAIN SLOWLY AND COMPLETE THE FOLLOWING QUESTIONS.

WHAT ARE SOME THINGS IN LIFE YOU FEEL ANXIOUS REGARDING? MAKE A LIST.

NOW "PRESENT YOUR REQUESTS TO GOD." OFFER YOUR ANXIETIES TO HIM AND ASK FOR FREEDOM AND HEALING, WITH THANKSGIVING, BELIEVE THAT GOD HEARS YOUR PRAYERS.

FINALLY, MAKE A LIST OF TWENTY THINGS YOU ARE GRATEFUL FOR. WORK HARD TO WRITE DOWN TWENTY—YOU MAY EVEN WANT TO DO MORE!

PRAYER

THANK GOD IN PRAYER FOR THE THINGS YOU LISTED AND COMMIT YOUR ANXIOUS THOUGHTS TO HIM.

REFLECTION AND REVIEW

O n the seventh day of each week, we're going to pause to review and reflect on the past week. If you are behind a day or two, use this day to catch up. If you are caught up, use this day to review the previous six days' notes—especially all the Scripture references and stories. Use these seventh days to review your responses and prayers as well.

WRITE A PRAYER BEGINNING WITH

GOD, THANK YOU

BASED ON YOUR WEEK'S READING AND
REFLECTION, READ THIS VERSE AGAIN AND
ANSWER THE FOLLOWING QUESTIONS.

THESE WERE ALL COMMENDED FOR THEIR
FAITH, YET NONE OF THEM RECEIVED WHAT
HAD BEEN PROMISED.

—HEBREWS 11:39

WHAT WERE THE MOST SIGNIFICANT THINGS
YOU LEARNED ABOUT GOD'S FAITHFULNESS
AND THE CHRISTIAN LIFE THIS WEEK?

WHAT WAS THE MOST SIGNIFICANT THING YOU
LEARNED ABOUT THE LONG "ULTRA-MARATHON"
WALK OF FAITH THIS WEEK?

WHAT WAS THE MOST SIGNIFICANT
THING YOU LEARNED ABOUT YOURSELF
THIS WEEK? WHERE DO YOU SENSE GOD
INVITING YOU INTO DEEPER FAITH AND
TRUST IN HIM?

WHAT WOULD YOUR LIFE LOOK LIKE IF YOU
FULLY BELIEVED AND LIVED LIKE JACOB'S
WITNESS TO KEEP FIGHTING THIS WEEK?

THROW OFF THE WEIGHT

LET US THROW OFF EVERYTHING THAT HINDERS AND THE SIN THAT SO EASILY ENTANGLES.

—HEBREWS 12:1

ALL THAT HINDERS

n sports such as running, cycling, and swimming, every ounce matters.

In the original Greek marathons thousands of years ago, runners trained with leg weights and then removed them on race day. Many of them even ran in the nude or very little clothing to reduce unnecessary weight during the long run. (Thankfully that's not a thing anymore.)

These days, when marathon runners pick out their shoes, they're counting not in pounds but ounces. While most running shoes weigh ten to twelve ounces, some are as light as five ounces. Similarly, road bikes are counted in grams, an even smaller margin; carbon road-bike frames are advertised to racers as weighing about two hundred to three hundred grams less than aluminum-frame bikes. That's a difference of half a pound! And while swimmers don't worry as much about weight, their "speed suits" are designed to minimize drag while cutting through the water.

The message is clear: If you're racing to win, you don't want anything weighing you down or holding you back.

THROW OFF THE WEIGHT

After the famous Hebrews 11 Hall of Fame that we looked at last week, the author begins Hebrews 12 by calling us to "fix our eyes on Jesus." But even before he does that, notice what he writes:

> THEREFORE, SINCE WE ARE SURROUNDED BY SUCH A GREAT CLOUD OF WITNESSES, LET US

THROW OFF EVERYTHING THAT HINDERS AND THE SIN THAT SO EASILY ENTANGLES. AND LET US RUN WITH PERSEVERANCE THE RACE MARKED OUT FOR US, FIXING OUR EYES ON JESUS, THE PIONEER AND PERFECTER OF FAITH.

—HEBREWS 12:1–2

As we prepare to run the race marked out for us, fixing our eyes on Jesus, we must first "throw off everything that hinders and the sin that so easily entangles." Let's look at each of these phrases in detail.

THROW OFF

To throw off something is to identify the source of weight or drag that is slowing you down or holding you back, and to take the initiative to take it off, cut it away, or replace it with something lighter.

As Kyle writes, "And yes, 'throwing off' implies something is on you. You can only know that something's on you if you feel it, experience it, or see its effects. The challenge is to identify these things in your life that are weighing you down and take action so that you will not grow weary and lose heart." (81)

EVERYTHING THAT HINDERS

What are we to throw off? First, "everything that hinders." Be specific in what weights or sources of drag need to be eliminated. What unnecessary weights might be holding you down? Even a small weight or a bit of extra drag can have a significant negative impact on your long run of faith.

Here are some examples to consider:
• Anxiousness: "Everything will go wrong."
• Unhealthy relationships: "No one really cares about me."
• Fear of rejection: "Everyone will hate me."
• Guilt over past mistakes: "I always do this."
• Misplaced shame: "There's something wrong with me."

SIN THAT ENTANGLES

Of course, not all the things described above are sins. We might rightly feel angry when someone or something we love is hurt, and we might feel anxious or worried in a situation that may cause us harm. When another person consistently mistreats us, it may be wise to "throw off" the relationship.

But much of what hinders us is rooted in the sin of pride. This pride can be displayed in many ways:

• Anger: "If everyone would just listen to me."
• Lust: "I should get whatever I want."
• Greed: "I should be able to have it all."

- Self-sufficiency: "I should be able to do it all."
- Envy: "They don't deserve that—I do."

The author of Hebrews is wisely instructing us to throw off everything that hinders and the sin that so easily entangles us. Why? He wants to encourage us, to put "courage in" us.

Kyle summarizes this well:

"Sometimes we think we need comfort when what we really need is courage. This is what we've learned so far. Sometimes what we want is sympathy when what we're really missing is strength. Sometimes we want someone to feel sorry for us when what we really need is someone to challenge us." (79)

This life is not a casual weekend race; this is a serious run for your life. Identify the weights slowing you down! Throw off the drag that holds you back! Don't give up!

DOODLE HERE

CONTENT AND MEANING

READ HEBREWS 12:1-3 AGAIN AND COMPLETE THE FOLLOWING EXERCISE.

WHAT ARE THE KEYWORDS AND PHRASES IN THESE VERSES? DESCRIBE WHAT EACH ONE MEANS IN CONTEXT:

SINCE WE ARE SURROUNDED BY SUCH A GREAT CLOUD OF WITNESSES:

LET US THROW OFF:

EVERYTHING THAT HINDERS:

THE SIN THAT SO EASILY ENTANGLES:

LET US RUN WITH PERSEVERANCE:

THE RACE MARKED OUT FOR US:

FIXING OUR EYES ON JESUS:

MEDITATION AND APPLICATION

READ HEBREWS 12:1–2 AGAIN SLOWLY AND ANSWER THE FOLLOWING QUESTIONS.

REVIEW THE LIST OF THINGS UNDER THE HEADING "EVERYTHING THAT HINDERS." WHAT RESONATES MOST PERSONALLY? WHAT WOULD YOU ADD TO THE LIST?

NEXT, REVIEW THE LIST OF EXAMPLES UNDER THE HEADING "SIN THAT ENTANGLES." WHERE DO YOU FEEL SOME CONVICTION?

BASED ON YOUR RESPONSES TO THE LAST TWO QUESTIONS, WHAT WILL IT LOOK LIKE FOR YOU TO THROW OFF THESE THINGS?

YER

?FULLY ASK GOD YOUR FATHER TO SHOW YOU WHAT ARE HINDERING YOU AND ANY SINS THAT ARE JG YOU. PRAY FOR A SOFT HEART AND STRONG THE LONG-DISTANCE RACE OF FAITH.

FREEDOM FROM ANXIETY

nxiety is a respecter of no one.

We all feel anxiousness, worry, and fear to one degree or another. Our experiences are all personal and unique, but many of the symptoms are shared: nervousness, racing thoughts, disrupted breathing, irritability, sleeplessness, headaches, forgetfulness, sadness, loneliness, and chronic pain.

One psychologist has noted that "the average American child today exhibits the same level of anxiety as the average psychiatric patient did in the 1950s" (Idleman 85–86). What do we do with our anxiety? Perhaps, like me, you're becoming more anxious just thinking about all this anxiety!

UNHINDERED

The Holy Scriptures often call us to throw off anxiety:
- "Do not worry about your life" (Matthew 6:25).
- "Don't be anxious about anything" (Philippians 4:6).
- "Cast all your anxiety on God" (1 Peter 5:7).

Let's be clear about this: Jesus is not condemning your anxiety; he's inviting you into a deeper life in him, where you can have freedom from anxiety. Indeed, many commentators believe the most accurate translation of Jesus' words in Matthew 6 reads, "You no longer have to be anxious."

Even though we all feel common anxiety symptoms, there's a wide range of how much we experience. If you struggle from clinical anxiety, characterized by a biochemical imbalance in your body's response to stress, you don't need to hear condemnation; you need hope. The Scripture on worry and any primarily desc al, everyday point us to trust in God. Trust in God doesn't mean you can't seek practical and medical relief from anxiety symptoms. Instead, you can trust God's good gift of grace. On this side of eternity, you may continue to have anxiety symptoms, but through trust in God, life-giving counsel, and a faithful community, you can be unhindered from anxiety.

Kyle writes, "Wherever you are on the anxiety spectrum, I believe God wants to take away the weight you've been carrying. If you could learn to hand it over to him, it would change the way you run your race. Imagine feeling strong, loose, and free rather than straining under a burden." (87)

TRANSFER THE WEIGHT

Consider 1 Peter 5:7 again: "Cast all your anxiety on him, for he cares for you."

This is a precious invitation. The verb cast here is not implying a release, such as merely casting away a fishing line. Instead, Peter is telling us to transfer the weight, as if transferring the weight of a fishing lure out into the sea. Consider how this changes the reading:

Transfer all your anxiety onto God—because he cares for you!

As Kyle summarizes, "Let God carry the weight that has been holding you back and keeping you down. What are you holding on to that you need to transfer over to God?" (90)

"CAST ALL YOUR ANXIETY ON HIM, FOR HE CARES FOR YOU."

—1 PETER 5:7

CONTENT AND MEANING

READ MATTHEW 6:25-34 AND COMPLETE THE FOLLOWING EXERCISE.

WHY DO YOU THINK JESUS USES THE PHRASE "DO NOT WORRY" (OR "DO NOT BE ANXIOUS") THREE TIMES IN THIS PASSAGE?

WHY DOES JESUS REFERENCE THE NATURAL WORLD— BIRDS IN THE AIR AND FLOWERS IN THE FIELD?

WHAT DOES JESUS PROPOSE WE DO INSTEAD OF CARRYING THE WEIGHT OF ANXIETY AND WORRY? (LOOK TO VERSES 33-34.)

MEDITATION AND APPLICATION

READ 1 PETER 5:7 AGAIN SLOWLY AND ANSWER THE FOLLOWING QUESTIONS.

WHAT ARE SOME "WEIGHTS" CAUSING YOU ANXIETY RIGHT NOW? THINK ALONG THE FOLLOWING CATEGORIES:

THE UNKNOWN: "WHAT IF _____ HAPPENS?"

THE UNLIKELY: ANXIOUS FEELINGS BASED ON RUMORS AND POTENTIAL

THE UNCONTROLLABLE: ANYTHING YOU LACK THE ABILITY TO CONTROL

WHAT WOULD IT LOOK LIKE TO "TRANSFER" THESE ANXIOUS THOUGHTS ONTO YOUR GOOD AND LOVING FATHER?

PRAYER

ASK THE FATHER TO SHOW YOU THE WORRIES AND ANXIETIES OF YOUR HEART. PRAY THAT HE WOULD ENABLE YOU TO TRANSFER THESE HEAVY BURDENS OVER TO HIM AND TO RECEIVE HIS PEACE AND FREEDOM INSTEAD. YOU MAY WANT TO PRAY WITH YOUR HANDS OUT AND YOUR PALMS UP, SIGNIFYING A POSTURE OF GIVING ANXIOUSNESS OVER TO HIM.

LONGING FOR A BETTER COUNTRY

et's turn our attention back to Hebrews 11. The chapter is a biography series—stories of those who put off their immediate desires and put their hope in *what was to come.*

LOOKING AHEAD TO ETERNITY

Abraham kept faith in God's promises, even though it meant waiting decades and dying without seeing their complete fulfillment. What sustained his faith? Hebrews 11 says "he was looking forward to the city with foundations, whose architect and builder is God" (v. 10).

Hebrews 11:13–16 describes these Old Testament saints together:

ALL THESE PEOPLE WERE STILL LIVING BY FAITH WHEN THEY DIED. THEY DID NOT RECEIVE THE THINGS PROMISED; THEY ONLY SAW THEM AND WELCOMED THEM FROM A DISTANCE, ADMITTING THAT THEY WERE FOREIGNERS AND STRANGERS ON EARTH. PEOPLE WHO SAY SUCH THINGS SHOW THAT THEY ARE LOOKING FOR A COUNTRY OF THEIR OWN … A BETTER COUNTRY—A HEAVENLY ONE.

THEREFORE GOD IS NOT ASHAMED TO BE CALLED THEIR
GOD, FOR HE HAS PREPARED A CITY FOR THEM.

—HEBREWS 11:13–16

Hebrews 11:39–40 goes on to list many others—faithful women and men who were mocked, beaten, and killed for their faith: "These were all commended for their faith, yet none of them received what had been promised, since God had planned something better for us so that only together with us would they be made perfect."

Do you see the connection?

• Abraham endured a long journey because he was looking forward to an *eternal* city.

• The Israelites endured their wandering expedition because they were looking ahead to an *eternal* country.

• Many others endured suffering and death because they were looking ahead to something *eternally* better.

TAKE THE LONG VIEW

In each of these examples, the women and men of faith were focused not merely on what they could see directly in front of them. They were looking ahead with eyes of faith. They could see long distance. They had an eternal vision.

Seeing long distance frees us from looking too much at ourselves and our current circumstances.

Pride, on the other hand, is nearsighted. When pride is active in our hearts, we become completely absorbed in our own circumstances and worries. As Kyle writes:

"Pride makes me self-centered. The more self-centered I am, the more I'm concerned about my own pleasures, desires, and comfort.

Pride refuses to ask for help. ... Chances are, you have some people in your life who would want to help you. It's just that you can't bring yourself to ask.

Pride has control issues. ... Pride makes demands and keeps us awake at night going over them. Pride tries to take control; humility trusts that God cares and is capable, and transfers the weight over to him." (96–99)

In every form, pride makes us nearsighted when we need to be far-sighted, even eternal-sighted.

Perhaps the single best example of looking forward to eternity is sitting in the center of Hebrews 11: The witness of Moses. We'll look at the farsightedness of Moses tomorrow.

CONTENT AND MEANING

REREAD THE EXCERPTS FROM HEBREWS 11 AT THE BEGINNING OF THIS DAY AND ANSWER THE FOLLOWING QUESTIONS.

IN WHAT WAYS ARE THE CIRCUMSTANCES OF ABRAHAM'S LIFE AND THE LIVES OF THE ISRAELITES DESCRIBED IN VERSES 13-16 AND 39-40 SIMILAR? IN WHAT WAYS ARE THE CIRCUMSTANCES DIFFERENT?

HOW DO YOU SEE THESE WOMEN AND MEN OF FAITH ACTING WITH A FORWARD-LOOKING FAITH, AND HOW DID IT SUSTAIN THEIR EARTHLY JOURNEY?

MEDITATION AND APPLICATION

REFLECT ON AND RESPOND TO THE FOLLOWING QUESTIONS.

WHAT IS ONE THING ABOUT YOUR SITUATION OR CIRCUMSTANCES RIGHT NOW THAT YOU'D LIKE TO HAVE CHANGED?

HOW MIGHT THIS SITUATION OR CIRCUMSTANCE BE SERVING TO PUT YOUR HOPE IN THE ETERNAL LIFE THAT IS TO COME?

WHICH OF THE THREE EXAMPLES OF PRIDE LISTED IN KYLE'S BOOK BEST FITS YOU? HOW HAS THIS FORM OF PRIDE THREATENED TO MAKE YOU NEARSIGHTED?

PRAYER

PRAY TO GOD THAT HE WOULD MINISTER TO YOUR HEART IN A WAY THAT IDENTIFIES AND UPROOTS PRIDE, REVEALS TO YOU HOW YOU MAY BE LIVING FOR THE MOMENT, AND REFOCUSES YOUR GAZE TO THE BETTER, ETERNAL LIFE THAT IS AHEAD OF US.

LOOKING AHEAD: THE WITNESS OF MOSES

I n the long-distance walk of faith, we need real encouragement—not generic, fluffy, simplistic platitudes. We need courage in our hearts—to give us strength, motivate our lives, and move us along.

In the witness of Moses, we find deep, gritty, life-and-death encouragement. The message of Moses for us today is, "Keep looking ahead!"

ON HOLY GROUND

Moses was an Israelite, but he was abandoned as a baby to avoid certain death. Taken in by Pharaoh's daughter in Egypt, he grew up privileged; his life was far better than his fellow Israelites. But to be clear, Moses was not a shining example of faith and self-control early in life. He killed an Egyptian who was being rough with an Israelite, so Pharaoh sought to capture him and put him to death.

So here we have another Israelite guilty and on the run, as Jacob was. Moses is definitively not the sort of fellow we expect to become the leader of God's people and a hero in the faith. But God appeared to him, and the transformation began.

While pursuing a lost sheep on the mountain of Horeb, Moses came upon a bush on fire. Immediately, a voice cried out to him, "Moses! Moses!" (Exodus 3:4). God, speaking audibly to Moses through the burning bush, continued, "Do not come any closer. Take off your sandals, for the place you are standing is holy ground" (v. 5). What could God possibly want with an ordinary, unimpressive shepherd like Moses?

THE LORD SAID, "I HAVE INDEED SEEN THE
MISERY OF MY PEOPLE IN EGYPT. I HAVE
HEARD THEM CRYING OUT BECAUSE
OF THEIR SLAVE DRIVERS, AND I AM
CONCERNED ABOUT THEIR SUFFERING. SO I
HAVE COME DOWN TO RESCUE THEM FROM
THE HAND OF THE EGYPTIANS AND TO BRING
THEM UP OUT OF THAT LAND INTO A GOOD
AND SPACIOUS LAND, A LAND FLOWING
WITH MILK AND HONEY. ... SO NOW, GO. I AM
SENDING YOU TO PHARAOH TO BRING MY
PEOPLE THE ISRAELITES OUT OF EGYPT."

—EXODUS 3:7–10

WHO AM I, LORD?

Moses's response is not far from how I would respond to a
divine invitation. Who, me? Certainly not! You must have the
wrong guy. I'm a nobody. I'm a murderer, in fact. I can't go back
there. Surely there's been some mistake!

But God insists, "I will be with you. And this will be the sign to
you that it is I who have sent you: When you have brought the
people out of Egypt, you will worship God on this mountain"
(Exodus 3:12).

That's all? You'll be with me?

Moses probably had two things running through his mind. First, Moses had a speech impediment; he was not a good fit for the vocal leadership of two million Israelites and several appearances in front of the king of Egypt. Second, he had a good, safe life now. He had a wife, kids, and a small flock to tend. Why rush into such a dangerous mission?

Moses may have thought all these things—but he still obeyed. And that's why the author of Hebrews includes him in the Hall of Faith.

MOSES CHOSE TO BE MISTREATED ALONG WITH THE PEOPLE OF GOD RATHER THAN TO ENJOY THE FLEETING PLEASURES OF SIN. HE REGARDED DISGRACE FOR THE SAKE OF CHRIST AS OF GREATER VALUE THAN THE TREASURES OF EGYPT, BECAUSE HE WAS LOOKING AHEAD TO HIS REWARD.

—HEBREWS 11:25–26

There it is: Moses was looking ahead. We'll look at this in more detail tomorrow.

QUESTIONS FOR REFLECTION

CONTENT AND MEANING

READ EXODUS 3:1-22 AND ANSWER THE FOLLOWING QUESTIONS.

WHY DOES GOD TELL MOSES TO TAKE OFF HIS SANDALS? WHAT DOES THIS MEAN AND REPRESENT ABOUT GOD?

WHY DO YOU THINK GOD CHOSE MOSES OF ALL PEOPLE TO LEAD HIS PEOPLE OUT OF SLAVERY IN EGYPT?

WHY DOES MOSES ASK WHAT GOD'S NAME IS, AND WHAT IS IMPORTANT ABOUT GOD'S RESPONSE?

MEDITATION AND APPLICATION

READ HEBREWS 11:23-29 AND RESPOND TO THE FOLLOWING QUESTIONS.

IN WHAT WAYS DO YOU RESONATE WITH MOSES'S INITIAL RESPONSE TO GOD (EXODUS 3:11)? WHAT ARE SOME THINGS YOU FEEL LIKE EXCLUDE YOU FROM SERVING GOD IN A SIGNIFICANT WAY?

HOW DOES IT ENCOURAGE YOU THAT MOSES CHOSE TO BE MISTREATED WITH THE ISRAELITES WHEN HE COULD HAVE ENJOYED A LIFE OF EASE?

WHAT IN YOUR LIFE NEEDS TO BE "THROWN OFF," IN ORDER TO FULLY EMBRACE GOD'S CALL ON YOUR LIFE? WHAT DOES IT MEAN FOR YOU TO CHOOSE SACRIFICE AND LOOK AHEAD TO YOUR ETERNAL REWARD?

PRAYER

OFFER A PRAYER OF THANKSGIVING THAT GOD HAS CALLED YOU HIS OWN AND GIFTED YOU TO DO ALL HE HAS SET BEFORE YOU. PRAY FOR INCREASED FAITH TO CHOOSE SACRIFICE AND EMBRACE GOD'S WILL FOR YOUR LIFE.

GREATER THAN TREASURES

Yesterday, we saw that Moses, after a fiery encounter with God on the mountain, chose to give up a life of ease and status in order to be persecuted along with the people of God.

Once more, Hebrews 11 summarizes Moses's faith:

> MOSES CHOSE TO BE MISTREATED ALONG WITH THE PEOPLE OF GOD RATHER THAN TO ENJOY THE FLEETING PLEASURES OF SIN. HE REGARDED DISGRACE FOR THE SAKE OF CHRIST AS OF GREATER VALUE THAN THE TREASURES OF EGYPT, BECAUSE HE WAS LOOKING AHEAD TO HIS REWARD.
>
> —HEBREWS 11:25–26

Moses threw off the weights of comfort and success in this life because he was looking forward to a greater reward. He regarded disgrace in Christ as of greater value than status and approval from Pharaoh.

What does it look like to believe Christ is greater than all earthly treasures?

ETERNAL REWARDS

Moses was faced with a choice—live for this world, or live for the life that is to come?

We might feel uncomfortable with the idea of eternal rewards—especially since our faith is entirely by grace—but Jesus often encouraged his followers to look ahead to the age to come.

"TRULY I TELL YOU," JESUS REPLIED, "NO ONE
WHO HAS LEFT HOME OR BROTHERS OR SISTERS
OR MOTHER OR FATHER OR CHILDREN OR
FIELDS FOR ME AND THE GOSPEL WILL FAIL TO
RECEIVE A HUNDRED TIMES AS MUCH IN THIS
PRESENT AGE: HOMES, BROTHERS, SISTERS,
MOTHERS, CHILDREN AND FIELDS—ALONG
WITH PERSECUTIONS—AND IN THE AGE TO
COME ETERNAL LIFE."

—MARK 10:29–30

This is Jesus' message and the witness of Moses: Throw off everything in this fleeting, temporary world and fix your eyes on God, and you will receive far more in eternity than anything you get on earth.

Or as Hebrews 12 puts it:

THEREFORE, SINCE WE ARE SURROUNDED BY
SUCH A GREAT CLOUD OF WITNESSES, LET US
THROW OFF EVERYTHING THAT HINDERS AND
THE SIN THAT SO EASILY ENTANGLES. AND LET
US RUN WITH PERSEVERANCE THE RACE MARKED
OUT FOR US, FIXING OUR EYES ON JESUS, THE
PIONEER AND PERFECTER OF FAITH.

—HEBREWS 12:1–2

FIX YOUR EYES

One time when my wife and I were at the beach with our three boys, I gave them a test. I told each one of them to see how straight of a line they could walk in the sand. So my sons looked down at their feet and took slow, careful steps, trying to line each one up as perfectly as possible. But when they reached the end and looked back, their paths were anything but straight. They looked like the footprints of a drunk wobbler.

So I had them redo the challenge, but this time I had them pick a point off in the distance. I told them not to worry about their feet, to just walk right to that point. And of course, they walked in a straight line.

The point is that when we are worried about each individual step, we lose focus on what's ahead of us and have no long-range perspective.

This is the exact sort of thing Jesus is telling us to do: "Don't worry about your individual steps. Instead, fix your eyes on me. Seek first my kingdom and my righteousness. I am the Eternal, the True, the One and Only. All else fails. And if you fix your eyes on me, you'll have everything you ever need—now and for eternity."

FIX YOUR EYES

CONTENT AND MEANING

READ HEBREWS 11:23–29 AND 12:1–2 AND ANSWER THE FOLLOWING QUESTIONS.

BASED ON WHAT YOU KNOW OF MOSES'S LIFE, WHAT SORTS OF TRIALS AND CHALLENGES DID HE FACE AS GOD'S SERVANT AND ISRAEL'S LEADER?

IN WHAT WAYS MIGHT CHRIST'S KINGDOM BE AT ODDS WITH EARTHLY TREASURES? IN OTHER WORDS, WHERE MIGHT GOD CALL US TO GIVE UP SOMETHING GOOD AND TEMPORARY TO SUFFER NOW, BUT RECEIVE SOMETHING GREAT AND ETERNAL LATER?

WHICH OTHER WOMEN AND MEN IN THE HEBREWS 11 HALL OF FAITH FIT THIS DESCRIPTION—GIVING UP THE THINGS OF THIS WORLD FOR THE SAKE OF GOD'S ETERNAL KINGDOM?

MEDITATION AND APPLICATION

READ MARK 10:29-30 AND MATTHEW 6:33 AND RESPOND TO THE FOLLOWING QUESTIONS.

HOW DOES IT CHALLENGE YOU THAT FOLLOWING JESUS MIGHT MEAN GIVING UP THE APPROVAL OF FAMILY MEMBERS AND FRIENDS (MARK 10:29-30)?

WHAT WOULD IT LOOK LIKE FOR YOU TO "SEEK FIRST" THE KINGDOM OF CHRIST (MATTHEW 6:33) IN YOUR EVERYDAY LIFE?

HOW MIGHT YOU FIX YOUR EYES ON JESUS, MAKING HIM YOUR POINT OF PERSPECTIVE OFF IN THE DISTANCE, TO WALK THE NARROW ROAD OF FAITH? WHAT THINGS IN YOUR PERIPHERAL VISION ARE TEMPTING YOU TO STEP OFF COURSE?

PRAYER

PRAY A PRAYER OF CONFESSION: ASK GOD TO REVEAL TO YOU HOW YOU MAY BE LIVING FOR THIS CURRENT, FLEETING LIFE INSTEAD OF CHRIST'S ETERNAL LIFE. THEN ASK FOR FORGIVENESS AND SEEK GRACE TO BECOME SINGLE-MINDED IN YOUR PURSUIT OF GOD AND HIS KINGDOM.

THROWING OFF WHAT OTHERS THINK

The witness of Moses reminds us to live for an audience of One.

Moses chose following God over obtaining acceptance in Egypt. He sacrificed a life of comfort for a life of demanding, wandering leadership of God's grumpy people. He gave up the good things of this world for the great things of eternity.

To do all of that, Moses needed to throw off one final weight—the fear of what others think.

FEAR OF WHAT OTHERS THINK

Kyle gives us a few indicators that we might be living with the fear of what others think—or what he describes under the acronym FOWOT.

• You go along with what someone else wants but secretly resent it.
• You change your opinion based on what everyone else thinks.
• You are afraid of being seen as weird after voicing an idea.
• You read into what other people say or do.
• You have a hard time asking for help.
• You have a difficult time saying no.
• You are critical of others. (117)

As much as I hate to admit it, I struggle with FOWOT every day. I want my co-workers to think I am clever and hardworking, so I'm tempted to make myself seem smarter or to give the impression that I've been working more than I have. I want the members of my congregation to like my sermons and tell their friends how great I am. I even want strangers to think that I have it all together, so I'm embarrassed when I spill my coffee or trip over a curb. And I would rather go to the grave with my self-sufficiency than admit my need and ask someone for help.

There are a few problems with FOWOT. First, it's exhausting. It's no way to live. Internally, I know there's no possible way that I'm going to achieve and maintain the constant approval of others. And yet I, almost subconsciously, strive to present myself as accomplished, thoughtful, and self-controlled.

Second, it's damaging to my relationship with God. He doesn't love me more when I preach above-average sermons. He isn't impressed by my "half-truths" about how hard I work. He doesn't love me any less when I stumble over a crack on the sidewalk and look back like an invisible hand reached up from the earth and tripped me. Kyle writes:

"You are free from earning God's love. When you begin to understand his love and acceptance, it releases you from fearing what other people think. Then, when you are finally free from the heavy weight of that, you feel light and swift, ready to sprint, eager to get back up and fulfill the mission purpose of your life." (118)

In Christ, you are free. You are loved. You can roll the heavy weight of FOWOT off your shoulders. You can run the race. Don't give up!

QUESTIONS FOR REFLECTION

CONTENT AND MEANING

READ HEBREWS 12:1-2 AND ANSWER THE FOLLOWING QUESTIONS.

REFLECTING ON THE LIFE AND WITNESS OF MOSES, HOW DID HE THROW OFF WHAT OTHERS THOUGHT ABOUT HIM?

THINKING BACK TO YESTERDAY'S STUDY, HOW DOES JESUS INVITE US TO A LIFE BETTER THAN 'FOMO'? HOW DOES SEEKING FIRST HIS KINGDOM FREE US FROM FEAR?

MEDITATION AND APPLICATION

HEBREWS 12:1-2 CALLS JESUS THE "PIONEER OF OUR FAITH." HOW DOES JESUS' FREEDOM FROM FEAR INSPIRE YOU TO LIVE ACCORDINGLY?

MAKE A LIST OF FIVE EXAMPLES OF 'FOWOT,' FROM YOUR OWN LIFE. WHOSE APPROVAL DO YOU MOST SEEK? WHAT ARE YOU MOST AFRAID OF? WHY DO YOU THINK THESE THINGS ARE THE CASE?

PRAYER

PRAY TO THE FATHER FOR FREEDOM FROM FEAR AND APPROVAL-SEEKING. ASK HIM TO REMIND YOU OF HIS LOVE FOR YOU AND TO EQUIP YOU FOR A LIFE OF FAITH AND ENDURANCE.

REFLECTION AND REVIEW

On the seventh day of each week, we're going to pause to review and reflect on the past week. If you are behind a day or two, use this day to catch up. If you are caught up, use this day to review the previous six days' notes—especially all the Scripture references and stories. Use these seventh days to review your responses and prayers as well.

WRITE A PRAYER BEGINNING WITH

FATHER, REMIND ME

BASED ON YOUR WEEK'S READING AND REFLECTION, READ THIS VERSE AGAIN AND ANSWER THE FOLLOWING QUESTIONS.

LET US THROW OFF EVERYTHING THAT HINDERS AND THE SIN THAT SO EASILY ENTANGLES. —HEBREWS 12:1

WHAT WERE THE MOST SIGNIFICANT THINGS YOU LEARNED ABOUT GOD'S FAITHFULNESS AND THE CHRISTIAN LIFE THIS WEEK?

WHAT WAS THE MOST SIGNIFICANT THING YOU LEARNED ABOUT THE LONG "ULTRA-MARATHON" WALK OF FAITH THIS WEEK?

WHAT WAS THE MOST SIGNIFICANT
THING YOU LEARNED ABOUT
YOURSELF THIS WEEK? WHERE DO
YOU SENSE GOD INVITING YOU INTO
DEEPER FAITH AND TRUST IN HIM?

WHAT WOULD YOUR LIFE LOOK LIKE IF
YOU FULLY BELIEVED AND LIVED LIKE
MOSES'S WITNESS TO LOOK AHEAD TO
ETERNITY THIS WEEK?

OBSTACLE COURSE

WE DO NOT HAVE A HIGH PRIEST WHO
IS UNABLE TO EMPATHIZE WITH OUR
WEAKNESSES, BUT WE HAVE ONE WHO
HAS BEEN TEMPTED IN EVERY WAY,
JUST AS WE ARE—YET HE DID NOT SIN.

—HEBREWS 4:15

THE OBSTACLES IN YOUR RACE

I n this study, we're asking God to provide genuine, heart-level encouragement for the long-distance race of faith.

God is often answering us and leading us through his written Word. In the witnesses of the saints throughout his story, we discover life-giving inspiration. And this inspiration is not a blissful platitude, but a gritty, hard-won, tenacious inspiration. These men and women gave their lives for our encouragement.

Remember The Living Bible's translation of our main passage (Hebrews 12:1):

"Since we have such a huge crowd of men of faith watching us from the grandstands ..."

This cloud of witnesses—you're welcome to envision your favorite sports team's wild, face-painted, chanting and cheering enthusiasts here—is shouting, "Let's go! You're almost there! Don't give up!"

Why do we need this real-life, in-your-face encouragement? Because our journey of faith is not only a long-distance race; it's also an obstacle course.

WHY WE LOVE OBSTACLE COURSES

Over the last two decades, obstacle-course races and events have grown exponentially in popularity. Turn on the TV on a weeknight, and you may find American Ninja Warrior athletes—non-professional folks like you and me—climbing ladders, leaping over swinging obstacles, and climbing walls, all in front of a raucous, cheering crowd.

Races like the Tough Mudder and Spartan Race are

now offered in every major city in the country. Ordinary women and men willingly subject themselves to running miles while also having to crawl under barbed wire, climb monkey bars, and get blasted with fire hoses.

Or go to your local gym and you'll likely find people training through CrossFit. Everyday folks are flipping tractor tires, carrying sandbags, and climbing ropes—and they pay to do this.

Why do we love obstacle courses? I believe we love obstacle courses for two reasons. First, human beings are meant to live risky, bold lives of faith, attempting great things and "pouring out" our lives for the kingdom. Whereas previous generations got these thrills through military training and combat, few in our generation are either living for Christ's kingdom or serving in the army, navy, or marines. Instead, we need voluntary workouts like CrossFit, occasional obstacle races like Tough Mudder and Spartan, and TV shows like American Ninja Warrior.

Second, we have been created for community—we are relational beings made in the image of a triune God. So our thrill for adventure is incomplete if it is not shared with others with a common interest and enthusiasm.

We've been created to overcome obstacles together.

Kyle writes:

"The Bible doesn't tell us to mark out our race just the way we like it and run—it's been marked out for us, so we don't choose its difficulty level, nor do we receive a map of the obstacles that lie ahead. ... As you study through Scripture, you'll find that those who faithfully ran the race God marked out for them had to deal with one obstacle after another. The faith heroes faced significant and surprising obstacles." (167)

This week, we'll look at the obstacles faced by incredible men of faith, Nehemiah and Joshua, and gain real-life, blood-and-sweat inspiration for our own obstacle course.

DOODLE HERE

QUESTIONS FOR REFLECTION

CONTENT AND MEANING

READ HEBREWS 12:1-2 AGAIN AND ANSWER THE FOLLOWING QUESTIONS.

THINK BACK TO THE WITNESSES OF ABRAHAM, JACOB, AND MOSES THAT WE READ IN THE PREVIOUS WEEKS. WHAT OBSTACLES DID THEY FACE IN THEIR FAITH JOURNEYS?

HEBREWS 12:2 CALLS JESUS, THE PIONEER OF OUR FAITH. WHAT OBSTACLES DID JESUS HAVE TO FACE, AND HOW DOES HIS VICTORY OVER THEM SECURE YOUR SALVATION?

MEDITATION AND APPLICATION

CONSIDER THE FOLLOWING EXAMPLES OF OBSTACLES, WHICH ARE PRESENT IN YOUR OWN LIFE?

- INDIFFERENCE: "I JUST DON'T KNOW WHAT I COULD DO TO MAKE A DIFFERENCE."

- INSUFFICIENCY: "I DON'T HAVE WHAT IT TAKES."

- OPPOSITION: "THERE ARE TOO MANY PEOPLE AGAINST ME."

- SLOW PROGRESS: "THERE'S TOO MUCH LEFT TO DO."

HOW DO YOU THINK GOD IS INVITING YOU TO OVERCOME THESE OBSTACLES? WHOSE HELP OR PRAYER CAN YOU SEEK IN OVERCOMING THESE OBSTACLES AND FINISHING YOUR ENDURANCE RUN OF FAITH?

PRAYER

PRAY TO THE FATHER FOR CLARITY IN SEEING THE OBSTACLES IN FRONT OF YOU. PRAY FOR BOLDNESS AND FAITH TO STEP OUT IN COURAGE, WITH THE SUPPORT OF OTHERS, TO CONTINUE TO MOVE FORWARD IN YOUR FAITH.

KEEP BUILDING: THE WITNESS OF NEHEMIAH

I f anyone knows what it's like to face overwhelming obstacles, it's Nehemiah.

Nehemiah's life is told in the books of Ezra and Nehemiah. He was an Israelite in a foreign land, working as a head servant within the pagan Persian Empire, about five hundred years before Jesus' birth. His job included regular access to the king of Persia, so he had a unique position of perspective and influence that not many would want to lose.

And yet, his hometown was in ruins. Nehemiah had most likely never lived in Jerusalem, the City of God. It was more than one thousand miles away and had been mostly abandoned for more than a century. But when Nehemiah heard a report that the Holy City had been attacked once again—its walls and gates burned down, and its people left vulnerable to additional attacks—he was overcome with sadness and grief.

ENTERING THE RACE

Like Abraham, Moses, and many heroes of faith before him, Nehemiah could have remained in his position of safety and security and ignored the needs of his fellow Israelites. But God inspired him to act. Nehemiah knew he needed to enter the race marked out for him.

In yesterday's questions for reflection, we looked at four common obstacles, and Nehemiah faced all four in full measure:

Indifference: Nehemiah could have waited for someone else, someone closer to or with a better knowledge of Jerusalem, to step in and show Israel the way. He could have said, "It's too late now," or "I'm not the right guy for the job."

Insufficiency: Nehemiah had a unique position in Persia, but he undoubtedly was taking a risk by asking for a leave of absence to check on Jerusalem. Similarly, he had no resources of his own through which to restore Jerusalem. He could have said, "I don't have what it takes."

Opposition: Once Nehemiah decided he would try to help rebuild Jerusalem, he had constant resistance. The nearby tribes joked and laughed at his efforts. Outside leaders rallied to thwart his attempts. Even his own people doubted whether the job was worth the demand. Nehemiah could have said, "There's too much working against me."

Slow Progress: Lastly, even when Nehemiah was given resources and began the work, it began slowly and without the immediate look of success. He could have said, "I gave it a shot. It just wasn't meant to be."

Nehemiah could have said all these things. He may have even thought them over and over. But he didn't pack his bags and return to his royal position in the palaces of Persia. He didn't give in.

He didn't quit.

AND LET US CONSIDER HOW WE MAY SPUR ONE ANOTHER ON TOWARD LOVE AND GOOD DEEDS, NOT GIVING UP MEETING TOGETHER, AS SOME ARE IN THE HABIT OF DOING, BUT ENCOURAGING ONE ANOTHER—AND ALL THE MORE AS YOU SEE THE DAY APPROACHING.

—HEBREWS 10:24-25

CONTENT AND MEANING

READ HEBREWS 10:24-25 AND ANSWER THE FOLLOWING QUESTIONS.

THINKING OVER THE LIFE AND WORK OF NEHEMIAH, HOW DID HE SPUR OTHERS ON TO LOVE AND GOOD DEEDS AND STAYING ON MISSION TOGETHER?

QUESTIONS FOR REFLECTION

WHICH OF THE FOUR OBSTACLES WE TALKED ABOUT DO YOU THINK WAS MOST DIFFICULT FOR NEHEMIAH TO OVERCOME?

MEDITATION AND APPLICATION

WHERE DO YOU FEEL OVERWHELMED BY OBSTACLES IN YOUR PATH? HOW DOES NEHEMIAH'S WITNESS TO "KEEP BUILDING" ENCOURAGE YOU?

WHAT WOULD IT LOOK LIKE FOR YOU TO SPUR YOUR FRIENDS, FAMILY, OR FELLOW CHRISTIANS ON TO LOVE AND GOOD DEEDS, TO NOT GIVE UP MEETING TOGETHER, AND TO ENCOURAGE OTHERS IN THEIR FAITH?

PRAYER

THANK GOD THAT HE IS ALWAYS WITH YOU, NEVER LEAVES YOU, AND WILL NEVER FORSAKE YOU. ASK HIM FOR FRESH COURAGE AND STRENGTH FOR THE MISSION HE HAS CALLED YOU TO. READ NEHEMIAH 1 TO SPUR ON YOUR PRAYERS.

THE POWER OF LIES

In Nehemiah's mission to rebuild Jerusalem, he faced numerous obstacles. Indeed, he faced opposition on almost all sides, and he had to continually reject the lies that his enemies wanted him to believe.

While working on the wall, Nehemiah's enemies accused him of rebelling against the king (Nehemiah 2:19). These enemies mocked the Israelites' desire to worship in Jerusalem (4:2) and questioned the quality of his work (4:3). They started a rumor that Nehemiah was setting himself up as king (6:6). They even plotted to kill laborers while busy at work (4:11). Finally, they attempted to trap Nehemiah in the temple to kill him (6:12).

All of these threats and accusations were futile attempts to throw Nehemiah off course—to keep him from obeying the Lord and rebuilding the city. But so often, the threats and accusations of others live on as lies inside our minds.

UNLEASHED FROM LIES

In our own lives, we often believe lies and unknowingly live our lives according to false narratives. Do you resonate with any of these thoughts?

- I'll never be good enough.
- I've made too many mistakes.
- I'll never be able to stop.
- God doesn't really care about me.
- No one truly cares about me.

Kyle writes:

"If you believe those lies, you will give them tremendous power in your life, because when you believe a lie to be true, you give it the same power as if it were. Believing those lies will make it difficult to keep going. Believing those lies will make you want to give up." (125)

When we get on Facebook and Instagram, we see perfectly curated lives of happiness, meaning, and creativity. We're tempted to think, my life isn't that nice and neat. Surely something is wrong with me!

When we make a mistake—run up money on a credit card, snap at one of our kids, or get in trouble at work—we are tempted by another lie. We want to think, I can fix it myself and then we muster up all the strength we have to pull it together and get it right.

Other times, we feel hurt or minimized by others and think, I don't need this. I deserve to be happy! And then we are tempted to buy into the lie that we'll find happiness in a new purchase or another drink or an unhealthy relationship.

Regardless of how these lies enter your mind, they find their root in our enemy, Satan, who is a thief and a liar, always trying to outwit and devour us (John 10:10; John 8:44; 2 Corinthians 2:11; 1 Peter 5:8).

Our lives of faith are obstacle-course races, and lies are all around us, threatening to pull us off course, drag us down, and keep us from finishing. Kyle encourages us to remember this truth: "With God, I have everything I need to do everything I need to do." (128)

QUESTIONS FOR REFLECTION

CONTENT AND MEANING

READ NEHEMIAH 6:1-9 AND ANSWER THE FOLLOWING QUESTIONS.

HOW DOES NEHEMIAH KNOW HIS ADVERSARIES WERE SCHEMING TO HARM HIM? HOW DOES NEHEMIAH RESPOND TO THE LETTER THE ENEMIES BRING HIM?

WHAT WAS NEHEMIAH'S RESPONSE TO ALL THESE LIES AND THREATS (SEE VERSE 9)?

MEDITATION AND APPLICATION

READ THROUGH THE FIVE EXAMPLES OF LIES LISTED IN THIS DAY'S READING.

WHAT SPECIFIC LIES ARE YOU TEMPTED TO BELIEVE ABOUT YOURSELF, OTHERS, AND GOD? HOW MIGHT YOU BE LIVING ACCORDING TO LIES AND WRONGLY SEEKING HAPPINESS OUTSIDE OF GOD'S PLAN FOR YOU?

HOW CAN YOU REGULARLY EXPOSE YOURSELF TO THE TRUTHS OF GOD AND HIS VIEW OF YOU?

PRAYER

PRAY TO GOD THAT HE WOULD REVEAL THE LIES THAT SURROUND YOU. PRAY FOR WISDOM TO DISCERN REALITY FROM FALSEHOOD AND COURAGE TO, LIKE NEHEMIAH, REJECT THE LIES AND KEEP ON BUILDING FOR GOD.

MISSION ACCOMPLISHED

Nehemiah faced numerous obstacles and was tempted to believe lies, and the resistance to his work was significant. So what did he do to keep going? What steps did he take to keep moving forward? Where did he find the confidence to accomplish the mission?

FACE YOUR OBSTACLES

Kyle gives us a few encouragements as we face the obstacles in our own lives, and once again, Nehemiah's life and mission inform our own struggles.

Embrace the Obstacles: Nehemiah didn't back down, but went head first into his challenges. He didn't get negative, he didn't get cynical, and he didn't give up.

Persevere in Prayer: Nehemiah fell to his knees in prayer when he learned of Jerusalem's condition, and he persevered in prayer throughout his mission. He remembered who God is and kept his faith in God, not in himself or others.

Just Keep Building: Nehemiah understood that God was rebuilding his city—and the Israelites were simply his chosen instruments of construction. So he kept showing up and doing the work, and the city was rebuilt ahead of schedule.

MISSION ACCOMPLISHED

Just a few short months later, God's people were back in the Holy City, the City of David, rebuilding the temple and worshipping God together. Indeed, the whole project was completed in only fifty-two days! All because Nehemiah kept building.

But still, you may want to say, "It's too late. I don't have what it takes. There's too much working against me. I gave it a shot. Now it's time to give up." Where do we get the strength to combat the obstacles in our life?

WEAKNESS AND CONFIDENCE

The author of Hebrews—a few chapters before he calls us to look to the cloud of witnesses—anticipated our struggles in faith and endurance. He encouraged us to lift our eyes all the way to the throne:

> THEREFORE, SINCE WE HAVE A GREAT HIGH PRIEST
> WHO HAS ASCENDED INTO HEAVEN, JESUS THE SON OF
> GOD, LET US HOLD FIRMLY TO THE FAITH WE PROFESS.
> FOR WE DO NOT HAVE A HIGH PRIEST WHO IS UNABLE
> TO EMPATHIZE WITH OUR WEAKNESSES, BUT WE HAVE
> ONE WHO HAS BEEN TEMPTED IN EVERY WAY, JUST AS
> WE ARE—YET HE DID NOT SIN. LET US THEN APPROACH
> GOD'S THRONE OF GRACE WITH CONFIDENCE, SO THAT
> WE MAY RECEIVE MERCY AND FIND GRACE TO HELP US IN
> OUR TIME OF NEED.
>
> **—HEBREWS 4:14–16**

Jesus is our great high priest. He is the One who makes a way for us to enter the presence of a holy God. Priests gave the Hebrew people hope; they weren't perfect, but they could stand before God. And yet where the Old Testament priests still had their own sin, Jesus was entirely without sin.

Jesus experienced every trial and temptation and emerged untainted so that we have in him one who knows what it's like to experience weakness and can welcome us to the throne room in confidence. This is the paradox of walking with Jesus: In our weakness we can have confidence, because the victory doesn't depend on us; Christ has already passed the test, overcome the obstacles, thrown off the weights, and finished the race.

_____

DOODLE HERE

CONTENT AND MEANING

READ HEBREWS 4:14–16 AND ANSWER THE FOLLOWING QUESTIONS.

WHAT DOES IT MEAN THAT JESUS IS OUR GREAT AND FINAL HIGH PRIEST?

IN WHAT SENSE DID JESUS BECOME WEAK? WHAT ARE SOME OF THE TEMPTATIONS JESUS FACED IN HIS OWN LIFE?

WHY IS IT SIGNIFICANT THAT JESUS ENDURED THE SAME TRIALS AND TEMPTATIONS THAT WE FACE, YET DID NOT SIN?

MEDITATION AND APPLICATION

READ HEBREWS 4:14–16 AGAIN SLOWLY AND ANSWER THE FOLLOWING QUESTIONS.

CONSIDERING NEHEMIAH'S PRAYER LIFE, HOW ARE YOU ENCOURAGED TO INCLUDE MORE PRAYER IN YOUR ORDINARY WORK AND EVERYDAY LIFE?

WHAT WEAKNESSES DO YOU FEEL AS YOU THINK ABOUT YOUR LONG-DISTANCE WALK OF FAITH? HOW DO YOU THINK JESUS EXPERIENCED THOSE SAME WEAKNESSES?

PRAYER

PRAY TO JESUS CHRIST—THE PIONEER OF OUR FAITH AND OUR GREAT HIGH PRIEST. APPROACH HIS THRONE IN CONFIDENCE AND RECEIVE HIS GRACE AND MERCY. PRAISE HIM FOR HIS LIFE, DEATH, RESURRECTION, AND ASCENSION BACK INTO HEAVEN TO ACHIEVE YOUR SALVATION.

JUST WALK:
THE WITNESS
OF JOSHUA

Hundreds of years before Nehemiah rebuilt Jerusalem, before Jerusalem had even been established as Israel's spiritual capital, another man overcame many obstacles to put Israel in a good place.

Joshua is first introduced in the Scriptures as Moses's young servant and apprentice. After Moses died, Israel had big shoes to fill. Who could possibly step into Moses's role and lead Israel across the Jordan River and into the promised land?

I WILL BE WITH YOU

In Deuteronomy 34, Moses passes away, and Israel calls for a thirty-day period of grieving. After the time of grieving was completed, God called Joshua to enter the race.

NOW JOSHUA SON OF NUN WAS FILLED WITH THE SPIRIT
OF WISDOM BECAUSE MOSES HAD LAID HIS HANDS ON
HIM. SO THE ISRAELITES LISTENED TO HIM AND DID WHAT
THE LORD HAD COMMANDED MOSES.

—DEUTERONOMY 34:9

AFTER THE DEATH OF MOSES THE SERVANT OF THE LORD,
THE LORD SAID TO JOSHUA SON OF NUN, MOSES'S AIDE
… "NOW THEN, YOU AND ALL THESE PEOPLE, GET READY
TO CROSS THE JORDAN RIVER INTO THE LAND I AM ABOUT
TO GIVE THEM. … AS I WAS WITH MOSES, SO I WILL BE
WITH YOU; I WILL NEVER LEAVE YOU OR FORSAKE YOU. BE
STRONG AND COURAGEOUS."

—JOSHUA 1:1–2, 5–6

If I were in Joshua's position, I would be overwhelmed with fear and doubt. But notice that God's first words to Joshua are "I will be with you." Before God calls Joshua with "Be strong and courageous," he first builds him up with "I will never leave you or forsake you."

Do you see the pattern? God only calls us to enter the race once he has promised to lead us through to the end. He only tells you to get off the couch and get to work once he has already promised to be with you. Some of you need to hear the battle cry, "Be strong and courageous!" And yet others of us will be tempted to be strong in ourselves and find courage in our own abilities. To us, God reminds, "I will be with you."

JUST WALK IN

Joshua's entrance into leadership began with two formidable obstacles: the Jordan River and the city of Jericho. In Joshua 3, Israel forded the Jordan River, with more than two million people and the ark of the covenant, to enter the promised land. The people rightly paused and celebrated God's provision. But the next challenge was even more daunting.

In Joshua 5–6, God appeared to Joshua in a vision, telling him, "See, I have delivered Jericho into your hands" (6:2). In the most unusual way, God provided for his people. They didn't even have to fight. Instead, God told Joshua and the people to march around the city and shout—that's all.

All Joshua had to do was walk in. On the seventh day, on the seventh lap, at the sound of the trumpet, the Israelites shouted in victory. Immediately, the walls of Jericho collapsed, and Joshua and the men of Israel simply walked in and took over the city. Hebrews 11 tells the story succinctly: "By faith the walls of Jericho fell, after the army had marched around them for seven days" (v. 30).

Sometimes the obstacles seem so big and the walls appear so tall. But God reminds us that he is with us. Therefore, we can be strong and courageous. Sometimes all we have to do is walk in faith.

What obstacles are in your way? What mission has God called you to embrace? What is needed right now?

Kyle concludes, "Battlefields have no rest stops or nap times. The time is always now to do what needs doing, to defend the poor and the overlooked, the widows and orphans, the hurting and the helpless. We need to serve God with a sense of urgency." (183)

CONTENT AND MEANING

READ JOSHUA 1:1-13 AND 5:13-6:27 AND ANSWER THE FOLLOWING QUESTIONS.

WHY IS IT IMPORTANT THAT GOD MADE A PROMISE TO JOSHUA BEFORE HE GAVE A MISSION? WHAT OTHER EXAMPLES OF THIS CAN YOU THINK OF IN SCRIPTURE?

QUESTIONS FOR REFLECTION

WHY DO YOU THINK GOD PROVIDED FOR JOSHUA AND ISRAEL IN THIS WAY? WHAT WOULD THEY HAVE LEARNED IN THIS UNUSUAL PROVISION?

MEDITATION AND APPLICATION

READ HEBREWS 11:30 AGAIN SLOWLY AND ANSWER THE FOLLOWING QUESTIONS.

WHAT IS THE ROLE OF FAITH IN THE STORY OF JOSHUA AND JERICHO? HOW DOES IT MOVE YOU TO APPROACH YOUR OWN OBSTACLES WITH FAITH AND OBEDIENCE?

WHAT DOES IT LOOK LIKE FOR YOU TO STEP INTO THE BATTLE OF FAITH "WITH A SENSE OF URGENCY" TODAY?

PRAYER

THANK THE FATHER FOR ALWAYS BEING WITH YOU TO PROTECT YOU. THANK HIM FOR RECEIVING A MISSION FOR YOUR LIFE—TO HONOR HIM AND FOLLOW HIM IN ALL YOU DO. PRAY FOR INCREASED FAITH TO FACE THE OBSTACLES IN YOUR LIFE.

UNTANGLED FROM UNBELIEF

Nehemiah and Joshua are examples of world-changing faith in the face of adversity:

• When they were confronted with obstacles, they kept moving forward.

• When they were surrounded by lies, they chose to listen to the truth.

• When they were tempted to give up, they continued to believe and act on the promises of God.

Hebrews 11–12 calls us to look to them as heroes of faith. And according to Hebrews, "Faith is confidence in what we hope for and assurance about what we do not see" (11:1).

What, then, is the opposite of faith? And how do we flee from it?

THE OPPOSITE OF FAITH

Of course, the opposite of faith is sin, but Scripture doesn't treat sin gener-ically. God always gets specific and personal. Our sin "tangles" us up like a spider web, to use Kyle's analogy (139), and we must become untangled through our return to faith.

So be specific: What are the sins that are entangling you? If nothing comes im-mediately to mind, consider a few common sin webs:

• Love of money and possessions: Envying what others have and lacking contentment with your own stuff

• Control: Refusing to accept the limitations of life and becoming demanding of others

• Revenge/retribution: Seeking to return wrong for wrong to put someone down

• Pleasure: Filling your life

with quick rushes of comfort and relief
• Status: Gaining the approval of others through your role or performance

All of these sins share the same root. Kyle writes:

"[Sins] all start with something good and noble. You see, behind the snags and entanglement is something attractive, and that attraction calls out, deep down, to who we are. The issue comes when we abandon the place God has for those things and become enmeshed in an unhealthy attitude toward them." (143)

In fact, each of our sins tends to have a shared foundation of unbelief. Most accurately, the opposite of faith is unbelief. Unbelief is our unwillingness to trust God at his word. Unbelief is not waiting to see if the promises of God will come true. Unbelief is taking matters into our own hands because we trust ourselves more than God's goodness and power.

Jesus invites us to become untangled from our sins. He calls us to move out of the spider webs of unbelief and into an active, abiding relationship of trust in his Father. Jesus reminds us that his sacrifice on the cross is enough to forgive our sins, untangle our unbelief, and restore us to his Father.

Christ is our great high priest (Hebrews 4:14–16). He is our once-for-all sacrifice on the altar (Hebrews 10:19–21; 13:12). He is the mediator of the new covenant, setting us free from sin to eternal life (Hebrews 9:15). He is the reason we can draw near to God with the assurance of forgiveness (Hebrews 10:22).

Let's go to him in faith today with confidence in what we hope for and assurance of what we can't see.

QUESTIONS FOR REFLECTION

CONTENT AND MEANING

READ HEBREWS 11:1 AND ANSWER THE FOLLOWING QUESTION.

HOW WOULD YOU PUT THIS DEFINITION OF FAITH INTO YOUR OWN WORDS? HOW DO YOU SEE THIS DEFINITION OF FAITH ON DISPLAY IN THE LIVES OF ABRAHAM, JACOB, MOSES, NEHEMIAH, AND JOSHUA?

MEDITATION AND APPLICATION

**READ HEBREWS 9:15 AND 10:19-22 SLOWLY AND
ANSWER THE FOLLOWING QUESTIONS.**

WHAT SINS COME TO MIND WHEN YOU SLOW DOWN
TO CONSIDER YOUR WAYS, MOTIVES, AND HABITS?
HOW DO YOU SEE UNBELIEF IN GOD AND HIS
PROMISES AT THE ROOT?

WHAT DOES IT MEAN THAT JESUS WAS A "RANSOM"
FOR OUR SINS IN 9:15? HOW CAN YOU APPROACH
GOD NOW WITH "A SINCERE HEART AND THE FULL
ASSURANCE THAT FAITH BRINGS" (10:22)?

PRAYER

ASK THE LORD FOR FORGIVENESS AND RESPOND WITH JOY
AND GRATITUDE FOR SENDING HIS SON!

REFLECTION AND REVIEW

On the seventh day of each week, we're going to pause to review and reflect on the past week. If you are behind a day or two, use this day to catch up. If you are caught up, use this day to review the previous six days' notes—especially all the Scripture references and stories. Use these seventh days to review your responses and prayers as well.

FOR WE DO NOT HAVE A HIGH PRIEST WHO IS UNABLE TO EMPATHIZE WITH OUR WEAKNESSES, BUT WE HAVE ONE WHO HAS BEEN TEMPTED IN EVERY WAY, JUST AS WE ARE—YET HE DID NOT SIN. LET US THEN APPROACH GOD'S THRONE OF GRACE WITH CONFIDENCE, SO THAT WE MAY RECEIVE MERCY AND FIND GRACE TO HELP US IN OUR TIME OF NEED.

—HEBREWS 4:15-16

BASED ON YOUR WEEK'S READING AND REFLECTION, READ THIS VERSE AGAIN AND ANSWER THE FOLLOWING QUESTIONS.

FOR WE DO NOT HAVE A HIGH PRIEST WHO IS UNABLE TO EMPATHIZE WITH OUR WEAKNESSES, BUT WE HAVE ONE WHO HAS BEEN TEMPTED IN EVERY WAY, JUST AS WE ARE—YET HE DID NOT SIN. LET US THEN APPROACH GOD'S THRONE OF GRACE WITH CONFIDENCE, SO THAT WE MAY RECEIVE MERCY AND FIND GRACE TO HELP US IN OUR TIME OF NEED.

—HEBREWS 4:15-16

WHAT WERE THE MOST SIGNIFICANT THINGS YOU LEARNED ABOUT GOD'S FAITHFULNESS AND THE CHRISTIAN LIFE THIS WEEK?

WHAT WAS THE MOST SIGNIFICANT THING YOU LEARNED ABOUT THE LONG "ULTRA-MARATHON" WALK OF FAITH THIS WEEK?

WHAT WAS THE MOST SIGNIFICANT
THING YOU LEARNED ABOUT YOURSELF
THIS WEEK? WHERE DO YOU SENSE GOD
INVITING YOU INTO DEEPER FAITH AND
TRUST IN HIM?

WHAT WOULD YOUR LIFE LOOK LIKE IF
YOU FULLY BELIEVED AND LIVED LIKE
NEHEMIAH'S WITNESS TO KEEP BUILDING
AND JOSHUA'S WITNESS TO JUST WALK
THIS WEEK?

FIVE

RUN YOUR RACE

RUN WITH PERSEVERANCE THE RACE
MARKED OUT FOR US, FIXING OUR
EYES ON JESUS, THE PIONEER AND
PERFECTER OF FAITH.

—HEBREWS 12:1–2

TAKE HEART: THE WITNESS OF GIDEON

In this study, we're asking God to provide true, heart-level encouragement for the long-distance race of faith. We've seen from Hebrews 12:1 that life is a race that God marks out for us, a race with many obstacles and entanglements. We find the faith to run with confidence by fixing our eyes on Jesus and listening to the crowd of witnesses—those great women and men of faith who have gone before us.

In the witnesses of Old and New Testament faith, we find fresh courage for our own race. But if I'm honest, I often struggle with the stories of Abraham, Moses, and Joshua. They barely seemed to bat an eye when faced with enormous challenges. They simply obeyed God. Indeed, they are models of faith!

But there is one soul in the Hebrews 11 Hall of Fame we can all relate to, and his name is Gideon (Hebrews 11:32).

GIDEON'S TEST

Gideon's story begins shortly after Joshua's death. Like Moses, Joshua had been a man of great faith, enduring to the end and finishing the race. But when Joshua died, the generation after him did not know the Lord or his mighty deeds. Instead, the Israelites only did evil in the eyes of the Lord (Judges 2:10–11). By the time Gideon entered the scene, God's people were oppressed by the Midianites.

One day, Gideon was out in the fields, hiding his crops from the Midianites, when the angel of the Lord appeared to him and said, "The Lord is with you, mighty warrior" (Judges 6:12). To which Gideon sarcastically replied, "If the Lord is with us, why has all this happened to us?" (6:13). The Lord let Gideon know that he had been chosen to save all Israel, and again Gideon was skeptical: "How can I save Israel? My clan is the weakest in Manessah, and I am the weakest in my family" (6:15).

Perhaps you resonate with Gideon's doubt. *Me, Lord?* Surely there is someone better for the job! And there probably was. God's choice of Gideon to lead Israel makes it clear that the battle belongs to God, not mighty warriors.

Unsure of himself and whether this angel of the Lord could be trusted, Gideon devised a test: He placed a wool fleece on the ground and said if, by morning, there is dew on the fleece but not the surrounding ground—then surely God is with me. God was willing, and the next morning, it was as Gideon asked. Still hesitant, Gideon reversed the test: Tomorrow morning, if the fleece has no dew but the surrounding ground does—then surely God is with me. Again, God was willing, and Gideon awakened to a dry fleece and damp ground.

TAKE HEART!

It's safe to say that Gideon is not a traditional hero. Next, it is God who would test Gideon. Before the upcoming battle with the mighty Midianites, God told Gideon to send away twenty-two thousand soldiers, leaving only ten thousand left to fight. Next, in a move that surely shocked everyone, God told Gideon to send away all but three hundred soldiers. Three hundred soldiers! Meanwhile, the Midianite army was described as being innumerable, just as the sand on the seashore (Judges 7:12).

I bet you can guess what happened next. Despite being outnumbered at an unbelievable rate, Israel routed the Midianites. Following the Lord's directions, Gideon and his three hundred men surrounded the Midianites at night, then shouted and broke candle jars around the camp. The Midianites were so startled that they turned against one another and wiped each other out.

Many years later, a better Gideon would arrive, one who wouldn't test God but who was obedient to his every word. Jesus Christ, the truly mighty warrior, told his followers: "In this world you will have trouble. But take heart! I have overcome the world" (John 16:33).

The witness of Gideon is this: The Lord fights our battles, we need only be still (Exodus 14:14). In other words, take heart! In Jesus Christ, God has won our battles and overcome the world.

"IN THIS WORLD YOU WILL HAVE TROUBLE. BUT TAKE HEART! I HAVE OVERCOME THE WORLD."

—JOHN 16:33

QUESTIONS FOR REFLECTION

CONTENT AND MEANING

READ JUDGES 6-7 AND ANSWER THE FOLLOWING QUESTION.

HOW DO YOU SEE GIDEON CHANGE THROUGHOUT THIS NARRATIVE? WHY DO YOU THINK HE IS INCLUDED IN THE HEBREWS 11 HALL OF FAITH?

MEDITATION AND APPLICATION

READ JOHN 16:33 SLOWLY AND ANSWER THE FOLLOWING QUESTIONS.

HOW DO YOU RESONATE WITH GIDEON'S FEARS AND UNBELIEF THAT GOD WOULD USE HIM? HAVE YOU EVER FELT LIKE YOU WERE FAR TOO SMALL OR INSIGNIFICANT FOR A TASK GOD WAS CALLING YOU TO?

FACING HIS OWN DEATH, JESUS ENCOURAGES HIS FOLLOWERS TO "TAKE HEART!" WHY COULD HE SAY THIS WITH SO MUCH CONFIDENCE?

PRAYER

PRAY TO THE FATHER WHO CALLS AND EQUIPS US FOR EVERY GOOD WORK. PRAY FOR WISDOM TO KNOW WHICH BATTLES HE IS CALLING YOU TO ENGAGE AND WHICH TO AVOID. PRAY THAT HE WOULD GIVE YOU FAITH TO STAND WHERE YOU ARE ASKED TO STAND.

TAKE THE NEXT STEP

When we look at the ultra-marathon race of our spiritual lives, it's easy to be overwhelmed.

How do I know God will always provide for me? What if something tragic happens to my spouse or child or best friends? What if I lose my job or things just don't work out for me?

Sometimes, the most incredible act of faith is the simplest one: Just take the next step.

ONE STEP AT A TIME

My kids have an old children's book called *Little One Step*, and my youngest son, Jack, particularly enjoys it. In the book, three brother ducklings are making a long journey through the woods back to their mother, when the youngest duckling gets overwhelmed and sits down. "My legs feel wobbly," he says. He looks up at the tall trees and sees the long road ahead of him, and he doesn't think he can make it.

His older brother encourages him, "Just try this: Take one step and say 'One,' then take another and say, 'Step.'" It's a brilliant coaching move, and the little duck tries it a few times, walking around in a circle. Finally, at the end of the story, the youngest duckling is marching ahead of his duck brothers, one step at a time, saying "One ... step ... One ... step." Arriving at his mother, he declares himself "Little One Step" (James 2003).

"IF YOU JUST TAKE THE NEXT STEP, AND THEN THE NEXT STEP, AND THEN THE NEXT, YOU'LL EVENTUALLY CROSS THE FINISH LINE."

Professional runner Wesley Korir gives the same advice for completing marathons. When he doesn't feel right, when his foot is hurting or the course is more demanding than expected, he tells himself, "One step at a time. Just take the next step" (Idleman 187).

Indeed, it's good advice for our spiritual lives too.

Kyle writes, "If you just take the next step, and then the next step, and then the next, you'll eventually cross the finish line." (187)

Like the little duckling, we might look up at the tall trees and see the rolling hills ahead of us. We might see all the needs of the world and wonder how we can make an ounce of difference. It may seem like we are just a stalk of grain in a thousand-acre field of corn.

But, in the same way, the apostle Paul encourages us today: "Let us not become weary in doing good, for at the proper time we will reap a harvest if we do not give up" (Galatians 6:9).

QUESTIONS FOR REFLECTION

CONTENT AND MEANING

READ GALATIANS 6:9 AND ANSWER THE FOLLOWING QUESTIONS.

HOW DOES PAUL KNOW WE MIGHT BECOME WEARY IN DOING GOOD?

WHAT IS THE CORE MOTIVATION FOR US TO NOT GIVE UP?

MEDITATION AND APPLICATION

READ GALATIANS 6:9 AGAIN SLOWLY AND ANSWER THE FOLLOWING QUESTIONS.

NAME AN AREA OF YOUR LIFE WHERE IT SEEMS YOU DOING GOOD IS AN UPHILL BATTLE. WHY ARE YOU BECOMING WEARY? HOW DO YOU FIND HOPE AND STRENGTH IN PAUL'S WORDS?

THINKING BACK TO JESUS' WORDS IN JOHN 16:33, HOW CAN YOU FIND THE INNER STRENGTH TO CONTINUE TO LIVE AS JESUS LIVED AND FINISH THE GOOD RACE SET OUT FOR YOU?

PRAYER

PRAY THAT YOU WOULD HAVE SPIRITUAL ENERGY FROM THE FATHER TO KEEP GOING. ASK FOR THE GRACE TO TAKE THE NEXT STEP AND CONTINUE THE RACE OF FAITH.

HOLY FEAR: THE WITNESS OF NOAH

In our study of Hebrews 11–12, we have seen numerous examples of faithful believers who put their hope in what's unseen and eternal. They didn't trust their eyes, and they didn't listen to the voices around them. Instead, they looked to eternity and listened for the voice of God.

There's one more man of faith in Hebrews 11 to look at in our study, and you likely know his unique story already.

> BY FAITH NOAH, WHEN WARNED ABOUT THINGS NOT YET SEEN, IN HOLY FEAR BUILT AN ARK TO SAVE HIS FAMILY. BY HIS FAITH HE CONDEMNED THE WORLD AND BECAME HEIR OF THE RIGHTEOUSNESS THAT IS IN KEEPING WITH FAITH.
>
> —HEBREWS 11:7

IN HOLY FEAR

Could you imagine what it would be like to be told by God that certain and profound judgment was coming on the earth? And then to be told that you and your family alone will be saved—if only you will trust him in doing the most bizarre and public display of faith possible? That's the story of Noah.

When God told Noah to start building the ark, there was not a rain cloud in sight. Remember, they're in the Middle Eastern desert, miles and miles from any ocean or sea. Floods don't happen here!

But while the story of Noah and the flood is recorded in Genesis 6–9, the testimonies of Noah's faithfulness abound throughout Scripture. The prophet Ezekiel uses Noah as one of the three chief examples of faith in the Old Testament (Ezekiel 14:14, 20). The book of 1 Peter praises God's patience and Noah's faith in their deliverance from the flood (1 Peter 5:20; see also Hebrews 11:7). And in 2 Peter, the disciple returns to this theme of Noah's faith, concluding:

> FOR IF GOD … PROTECTED NOAH, A PREACHER OF
> RIGHTEOUSNESS … THEN THE LORD KNOWS HOW TO RESCUE
> THE GODLY FROM TRIALS AND TO HOLD THE UNRIGHTEOUS FOR
> PUNISHMENT ON THE DAY OF JUDGMENT.
> —2 PETER 2:4–5, 9

In each of these instances, Noah's faith in God's promises is set against the unrighteousness of his neighbors and the judgment they received for their wrongdoings. Noah is the Bible's prime example of this "holy fear" that Hebrews 11:7 describes: No matter how much others mock you, no matter how impossible the mission in front of you seems to be, continue to fear our holy God, for he is faithful to deliver you!

Jesus' own words show the only two paths by which we can walk:

> "ENTER THROUGH THE NARROW GATE. FOR WIDE IS THE GATE
> AND BROAD IS THE ROAD THAT LEADS TO DESTRUCTION,
> AND MANY ENTER THROUGH IT. BUT SMALL IS THE GATE AND
> NARROW THE ROAD THAT LEADS TO LIFE, AND ONLY A FEW FIND
> IT."
> —MATTHEW 7:13–14

In other words, there's a way that seems right to the world, but it ends in death (Proverbs 14:12), and there's a way that seems wrong to the world—it looks too serious, too spiritual, too righteous to be any fun—and it ends with eternal life.

So the witness of Noah is this: Take the road less traveled. Choose the narrow gate. Decide to keep your holy fear in the one true God. All other paths lead to death and destruction. As the old hymn goes:

"When all around this world gives way,
he then is all my hope and stay.
On Christ the solid rock I stand,
·ll other ground is sinking sand."

HYMN

THE SOLID ROCK

WORDS: EDWARD MOTE, 1834
MUSIC: WILLIAM B. BRADBURY, 1863

1. My hope is built on noth-ing less than Je - sus' blood and
2. When dark-ness seems to hide His face, I rest on His un -
3. His oath, His cov - e - nant, His blood sup - port me in the
4. When He shall come with trum-pet sound, oh, may I then in

righ - teous-ness; I dare not trust the sweet-est frame, but
chang-ing grace; in ev - ery high and storm - y gale, my
whelm-ing flood; when all a - round my soul gives way, He
Him be found, dressed in His righ - teous - ness a - lone, fault -

whol-ly lean on Je - sus' name.
an - chor holds with - in the veil. On Christ, the sol - id Rock, I stand; all
then is all my hope and stay.
less to stand be - fore the throne.

oth - er ground is sink-ing sand, all oth - er ground is sink-ing sand.

QUESTIONS FOR REFLECTION

CONTENT AND MEANING

READ GENESIS 6-9 AND ANSWER THE FOLLOWING QUESTIONS.

WHY DOES GOD CHOOSE NOAH TO BUILD THE ARK? WHAT IS IT ABOUT HIM AND HIS FAMILY THAT CAUGHT GOD'S ATTENTION?

WE TEND TO CRINGE AT THE THOUGHT OF GOD ALLOWING PEOPLE TO FACE JUDGMENT, BUT MAKE NO MISTAKE, JESUS AFFIRMS A COMING DAY OF JUDGMENT FOR ALL PEOPLE. READ MATTHEW 7:13-27 AND REFLECT ON THE THREE METAPHORS—TWO PATHS, TWO TREES, AND TWO FOUNDATIONS. HOW DOES THIS "HOLY FEAR" DESCRIBE NOAH'S RIGHTEOUSNESS?

MEDITATION AND APPLICATION

REFLECTING ON GENESIS 6-9 AND MATTHEW 7:13-27, ANSWER THE FOLLOWING QUESTIONS.

WHAT ASPECTS OF NOAH'S STORY CONNECT WITH YOU? DO YOU OFTEN FEEL MOCKED OR RIDICULED FOR YOUR FAITH? HOW CAN YOU RESPOND WITH THE PATIENCE AND WISDOM OF CHRIST?

WHEN JESUS CALLS US TO TAKE THE NARROW ROAD, WHAT COMES TO MIND? HOW CAN YOU HUMBLY ENTER THROUGH THE NARROW GATE AND BUILD YOUR HOUSE ON A FIRM FOUNDATION?

PRAYER

IN YOUR JOURNEY OF FAITH, PRAY THAT GOD WOULD ENABLE YOU TO EMBRACE A HOLY FEAR OF HIM AND HIS WORD SO THAT YOU MIGHT WITHSTAND TEMPTATION AND BE COUNTED AS RIGHTEOUS AT THE END OF THE AGE.

KEEP YOUR CONFIDENCE IN CHRIST

Throughout this study journal, we've been calling you to faith and endurance in your walk with Christ. The examples of faith from Hebrews 11–12 have provided a cheering crowd, urging you to "Keep going! Don't give up!"

But if these words of encouragement still feel like empty phrases of light platitudes, let's pause again and revisit the Scriptures. The only way you can keep going—your only hope to not give up—is to keep your confidence in Christ himself.

> CONSIDER [JESUS] WHO ENDURED SUCH OPPOSITION FROM SINNERS, SO THAT YOU WILL NOT GROW WEARY AND LOSE HEART.
>
> —HEBREWS 12:3

What does it look like to consider Christ? How do we keep our confidence in him?

CONSIDER COURAGE AND CONFIDENCE

It is often true that courage and confidence go together.

In chapter 10 of *Don't Give Up*, "Keep Your Confidence," Kyle describes the scene of a day spent with an elite military training force. When real soldiers came in to drive his team out of the training exercise, simulated gunshots rang out, and explosives (which were, of course, fake) filled the sky with fire and smoke. Kyle panicked and ran. Any of us would! (203-205)

The point is important: If we are unprepared for battle, we will have little confidence, and with little confidence, we have an even smaller chance of emerging unscathed. Just as being told to "be brave" without good reason and confidence is no use, we need real courage to come from a place of rock-solid reality.

Throughout the book of Hebrews, confidence is connected to the person and work of Jesus Christ. If we are to have real confidence anywhere, it should be in the Lord and Savior of the universe.

Our task, then, is to develop confidence for the real battle of life by considering Jesus Christ. To consider him is to dwell deeply on who he is and what he has done. Therefore, the writer of Hebrews says, "Consider Jesus."

- Consider how Jesus was opposed throughout his life.
- Consider how Jesus kept his faith steady in his Father's promises.
- Consider how Jesus never gave up on his friends and followers.
- Consider how Jesus went to the cross for our sins, though he was sinless.
- Consider how Jesus rose from the grave, in eternal victory over Satan, sin, and death.

How will you find the courage and confidence to keep moving forward, not to run away when things get dangerous and difficult? Consider Jesus! Get to know him. Give yourself entirely to him. In doing so, you will not grow weary or lose heart. The battle has already been won.

QUESTIONS FOR REFLECTION

CONTENT AND MEANING

READ HEBREWS 12:1-3 AND ANSWER THE FOLLOWING QUESTIONS.

WHAT IS IMPORTANT ABOUT THE CONTEXT OF HEBREWS 11 AND 12:1-2 IN HOW WE READ 12:3?

CONSIDER JESUS' EARTHLY LIFE AND MINISTRY. WHERE DO SEE STRENGTH IN HIS CHARACTER, POWER, AND MERCY?

MEDITATION AND APPLICATION

READ HEBREWS 12:3 AGAIN SLOWLY AND ANSWER THE FOLLOWING QUESTIONS.

WHERE IN LIFE DO YOU LACK CONFIDENCE? WHAT DOES IT LOOK LIKE FOR YOU TO CONSIDER CHRIST IN THAT PLACE?

CONSIDERING THE TRIALS AND OPPOSITION THAT JESUS FACED, HOW CAN YOU FIND, IN HIS LIFE AND FAITHFULNESS, FRESH COURAGE FOR TODAY'S TEMPTATIONS AND CHALLENGES IN HIS LIFE?

PRAYER

ASK THE LORD JESUS TO EMPOWER YOU WITH REAL AND STEADY CONFIDENCE THROUGH HIS SPIRIT. THANK THE FATHER FOR THE STRENGTH GIVEN TO YOU IN CHRIST.

FINISH WELL: THE WITNESS OF PAUL

Throughout this study, we've looked at the women and men of Hebrews 11 as "the cloud of witnesses" that encourage us and call us to action in Hebrews 12:1–3. But perhaps the best place to finish our study is with a faithful believer who was still alive during Hebrews 11's writing and embodies its strength as well as anyone.

SAUL: THE OLD MAN

It is often true that courage and confidence go together.

He was born Saul of Tarsus, but you may know him better as the apostle Paul. We meet the man when he was still Saul of Tarsus, the Pharisee and a fierce enemy to Christianity. Saul's opposition to the early church made Nehemiah's accusers look shabby. Saul was present and approving of Stephen's death by stoning (Acts 7:58, 8:1). He went house to house throughout Jeru-salem, dragging Christians out of their homes and putting them in prison (Acts 8:3). When he was finished in Jerusalem, he asked permission to go through the countryside and foreign places to find and imprison Christians. Luke, the author of Acts, describes Saul as "breathing out murderous threats against the Lord's disciples" (Acts 9:1).

That's when Saul met Jesus.

While pursuing Christians in faraway Damascus, Saul was blinded by a bright light along the road. This was no ordinary light, and it wasn't merely an angel. It was the Son of God, Jesus Christ, risen and ascended, appearing in glory to Saul on the road. Saul fell on his face, was blinded for three days, and was led by the hand to Damascus where he would finally submit to the Lord and begin to pray (Acts 9:1–28).

PAUL: THE NEW MAN

When Saul emerged from his retreat in Damascus, he was no longer Saul. Such a profound transformation had taken place, that his old name simply wouldn't do anymore. He was now Paul. Immediately he began to encourage the disciples and preach the good news of Jesus' resurrection.

Paul—by virtue of having a personal encounter with the risen Lord on the road—was given apostle status along with the original disciples. He was charged with leading the spread of the gospel and the planting of churches in the Roman world, everything outside of Jerusalem and Israel. Over the next few decades, he would plant hundreds of churches, be imprisoned many times, and write more than a dozen of the letters that remain in our New Testament today.

And most important for our study: Paul finished well.

Paul ran the race, he kept the faith, and he reached the end. Tomorrow, we'll look at his words of encouragement for a long life of faith and endurance in Christ.

QUESTIONS FOR REFLECTION

CONTENT AND MEANING

READ ACTS 7:58-8:3 AND 9:1-28, AND ANSWER THE FOLLOWING QUESTIONS.

WHY DO YOU THINK LUKE, THE AUTHOR OF ACTS, INCLUDES THE DESCRIPTION OF SAUL'S LIFE BEFORE HIS ENCOUNTER WITH JESUS? HOW DO YOU THINK THE BELIEVERS IN DAMASCUS WOULD HAVE RESPONDED TO THE NEWS THAT SAUL HAD BECOME A CHRISTIAN?

SAUL'S CONVERSION TO PAUL WAS UNIQUE AND DRAMATIC. WHAT STANDS OUT TO YOU FROM THE TEXT? WHAT IS SIMILAR TO ALL BELIEVERS' CONVERSION EXPERIENCE, AND WHAT ELEMENTS ARE UNIQUE TO PAUL'S ENCOUNTER?

MEDITATION AND APPLICATION

**READ ACTS 9:17–19 AGAIN AND ANSWER THE
FOLLOWING QUESTIONS.**

WHY DO YOU THINK GOD SENT ANANIAS TO MEET
WITH SAUL PERSONALLY? HOW DOES GOD MINISTER
TO SAUL THROUGH ANANIAS AND HIS CHURCH IN
DAMASCUS?

WHY IS IT SIGNIFICANT THAT "SCALES FELL FROM
SAUL'S EYES" (ACTS 9:18) AND THAT HE WAS
BAPTIZED IMMEDIATELY? THINKING OF YOUR OWN
CONVERSION AND BAPTISM, HOW WOULD YOU
DESCRIBE YOUR ENCOUNTER WITH JESUS AND THE
CHURCH?

THINKING ABOUT SAUL'S TRANSFORMATION TO PAUL,
HOW ARE YOU ENCOURAGED THAT THE LORD COULD
(AND LOVES TO) USE BROKEN, SINFUL PEOPLE TO
PROCLAIM HIS GLORY AND BUILD HIS CHURCH?

PRAYER

PRAY THAT GOD WOULD OPEN YOUR EYES AGAIN AND GIVE YOU
A VISION AND FRESH COURAGE TO KEEP RUNNING AND KEEP
FIGHTING IN YOUR FAITH.

ANCHOR FOR YOUR SOUL

Yesterday, we were introduced to Paul, the enemy of Christ turned apostle of Christ. After his long journey of faith and his courageous work in the expansion of Christianity, he found himself in a bleak place.

He was in prison, cold and alone, and facing execution. These were his final days. This time, there was no earthquake to throw open the jail cells. No angels were coming to his rescue. He didn't even have his friends with him. Lesser folks would have despaired and possibly even recanted the faith. But not Paul.

Paul picked up his pen and paper, and he wrote us a letter.

FINISH THE RACE

Technically, he wrote 2 Timothy to his young apprentice in the ministry, but its words hold true for all of us, even two thousand years later. Paul wrote:

FOR I AM ALREADY BEING POURED OUT LIKE A DRINK OFFERING, AND THE TIME FOR MY DEPARTURE IS NEAR. I HAVE FOUGHT THE GOOD FIGHT, I HAVE FINISHED THE RACE, I HAVE KEPT THE FAITH. NOW THERE IS IN STORE FOR ME THE CROWN OF RIGHTEOUSNESS, WHICH THE LORD, THE RIGHTEOUS JUDGE, WILL AWARD TO ME ON THAT DAY—AND NOT ONLY TO ME, BUT ALSO TO ALL WHO HAVE LONGED FOR HIS APPEARING.

—2 TIMOTHY 4:6–8

Paul's words for Timothy then are the same words I imagine he'd encourage us with today: Finish the race! Keep going. It will be worth it. Don't give up!

Reflecting on his life, he said with humble confidence, "I have fought the good fight, I have finished the race, I have kept the faith."

Further, Paul was elated to face his death, because it meant he would receive his reward—a crown of righteousness from his Lord and Savior, Jesus Christ. Finally, he would be back in the presence of Christ, but this time, he wouldn't be blinded and knocked off his high horse.

This time, he would be home.

Paul's words to us fit with the witnesses of Abraham, Jacob, Moses, Nehemiah, and Gideon, Noah, and the cloud of witnesses in Hebrews 11. Paul's witness is simple: Finish the race!

AN ANCHOR FOR OUR SOULS

To return to Hebrews, we can be sure—we can have faith, hope, and humble confidence—that God's promises hold true for us today.

> GOD [MAKES HIS PROMISES TO US] SO THAT ... WE WHO HAVE FLED TO TAKE HOLD OF THE HOPE SET BEFORE US MAY BE GREATLY ENCOURAGED. WE HAVE THIS HOPE AS AN ANCHOR FOR THE SOUL, FIRM AND SECURE.
> —HEBREWS 6:18–19

God's promises never fall to the ground. Those who have gone before us, the cloud of witnesses, all testify: God keeps his promises; therefore, have faith! Believe him. Trust him. Fix your eyes on him.

Keep running. Keep your confidence in Christ. Take hold of the hope.

Don't give up!

CONTENT AND MEANING

READ 2 TIMOTHY 4:6–8 AND ANSWER THE FOLLOWING QUESTIONS.

HAVING REACHED THE END OF HIS LIFE AND MINISTRY, WHAT IS ON PAUL'S MIND? WHY DOES HE WRITE TO TIMOTHY OF ALL PEOPLE?

HOW CAN WE FIND ENCOURAGEMENT AND STRENGTH IN PAUL'S FINAL WORDS TO TIMOTHY? WHAT IS THE "CROWN OF RIGHTEOUSNESS" THAT AWAITED PAUL?

MEDITATION AND APPLICATION

**READ HEBREWS 6:18-19 AGAIN SLOWLY, AND
ANSWER THE FOLLOWING QUESTIONS.**

WHAT DOES IT LOOK LIKE FOR YOU TO TAKE HOLD
OF THE HOPE SET BEFORE YOU? HOW ARE YOU
ENCOURAGED THAT GOD'S FAITHFULNESS TO HIS
PROMISES IS "AN ANCHOR FOR THE SOUL, FIRM AND
SECURE"?

ONE LAST TIME, WHERE IN YOUR LIFE ARE YOU
TEMPTED TO GIVE IN TO SIN, STEP OUT OF THE
RACE, OR GIVE UP THE GOOD FIGHT? HOW DO YOU
SEE CHRIST—AND ALL THE CLOUD OF WITNESSES—
CALLING OUT TO YOU TO KEEP GOING?

PRAYER
THANK THE FATHER FOR ANY NEW REFLECTIONS, COURAGE, AND
COMMITMENTS THAT HAVE EMERGED OVER THESE LAST FIVE
WEEKS. THANK HIM FOR THE ABILITY TO COMPLETE THE STUDY AND
PUT INTO PRACTICE ALL THAT YOU HAVE LEARNED. PRAISE HIM!

REFLECTION AND REVIEW

On the seventh day of each week, we're going to pause to review and reflect on the past week. If you are behind a day or two, use this day to catch up. If you are caught up, use this day to review the previous six days' notes—especially all the Scripture references and stories. Use these seventh days to review your responses and prayers as well.

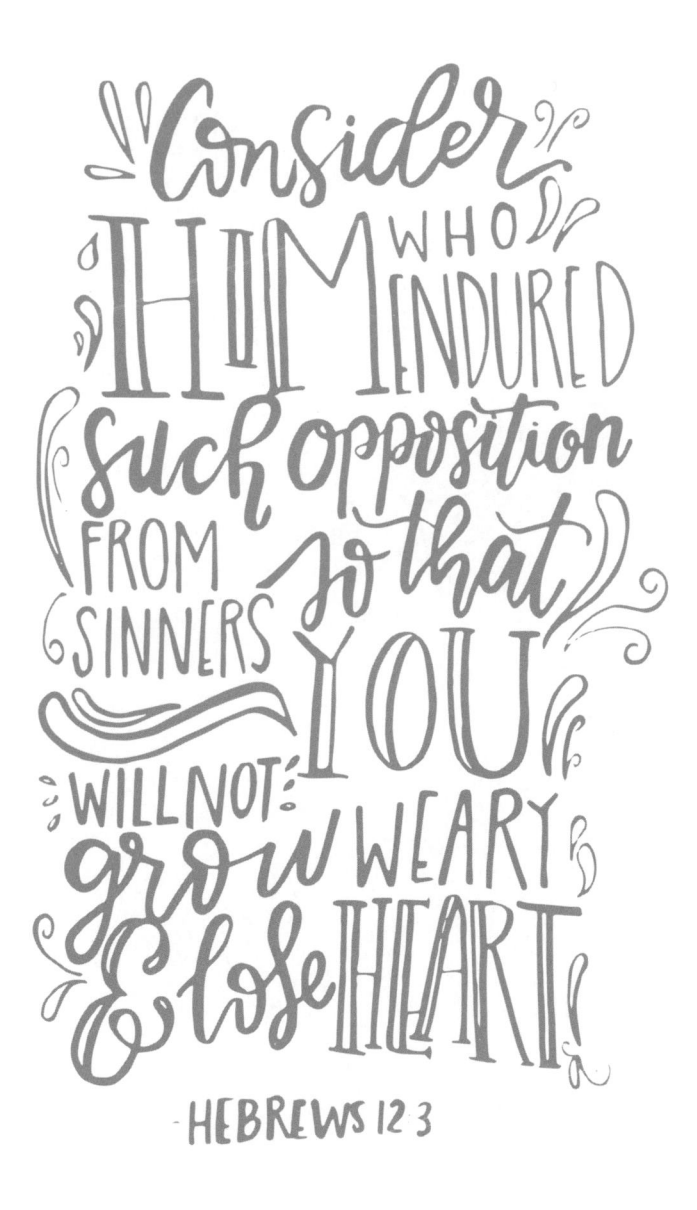

Consider HIM WHO ENDURED such opposition FROM SINNERS so that YOU WILL NOT grow WEARY & lose HEART

- HEBREWS 12 3

BASED ON YOUR WEEK'S READING AND REFLECTION, READ THIS VERSE AGAIN AND ANSWER THE FOLLOWING QUESTIONS.

RUN WITH PERSEVERANCE THE RACE MARKED OUT FOR US, FIXING OUR EYES ON JESUS, THE PIONEER AND PERFECTER OF FAITH.

—HEBREWS 12:1-2

WHAT WERE THE MOST SIGNIFICANT THINGS YOU LEARNED ABOUT GOD'S FAITHFULNESS AND THE CHRISTIAN LIFE THESE LAST FIVE WEEKS?

WHAT WAS THE MOST SIGNIFICANT THING YOU LEARNED ABOUT THE LONG "ULTRA-MARATHON" WALK OF FAITH THESE LAST FIVE WEEKS?

REFERENCES

Idleman, Kyle. *Don't Give Up*. Grand Rapids: Baker Publishing Group, 2019. Print.

"These Lightweight Running Shoes Are the Next Best Thing to Running on Air," *Runner's World*, October 3, 2018, https://www.runnersworld.com/gear/a20865752/best-lightweight-running-shoes/.

Frederick Dale Bruner, *Matthew: A Commentary. Volume 1: The Christbook, Matthew 1-12* (Grand Rapids: Eerdmans, 2007)

James, Simon. *Little One Step*. Somerville, Candlewick Press, 2003. Print.

Edward Mote, "The Solid Rock," 1834.

ABOUT THE AUTHOR

Jeremy Linneman

Jeremy Linneman, M.A., is teaching pastor of Trinity
Community Church in Columbia, Missouri. Prior to planting
Trinity, he served as a staff pastor of Sojourn Community
Church in Louisville, Kentucky, for seven years. He is
the author of *Life-Giving Groups: How to Grow Healthy,
Multiplying Community Groups*, and three other study
journals for City on a Hill Studios: *Grace is Greater, I Can
Only Imagine*, and *The End of Me*. His articles and resources
are available at jslinneman.com. He and his wife, Jessie,
have three sons and spend most of their free time outdoors.